The Logic of Action

FRANCES POCKMAN HAWKINS

The
LOGIC OF ACTION
Young Children at Work

Photographs and Notes by
Claire Ulam Grusin

Pantheon Books

A DIVISION OF RANDOM HOUSE, NEW YORK

All rights reserved under International and Pan-American Copyright Conventions. Published in the United States by Pantheon Books, a division of Random House, Inc., New York, and simultaneously in Canada by Random House of Canada Limited, Toronto.

Library of Congress Cataloging in Publication Data

Hawkins, Frances Pockman, 1913–
The Logic of Action.

Rev. ed. of a work first published in 1969 by the Elementary Science Advisory Center, University of Colorado.
Bibliography: pp. 143–44
1. Deaf—Education. 2. Open plan schools. 3. Teachers of the deaf. I. Title.
HV2430.H38   1974   371.9'12   74-5270
ISBN 0-394-49389-3
ISBN 0-394-70923-2 (pbk.)

Two short excerpts from "The Strange Case of the Blind Babies" by Theodore H. Ingalls, *Scientific American*, December, 1955. Copyright © 1955 by Scientific American, Inc. All Rights Reserved.

Manufactured in the United States of America
FIRST EDITION

Acknowledgment

I am grateful to so many friends and colleagues that I find it almost impossible to select out names. I have tried, but like the little old man in Wanda Gag's *Millions of Cats* I end by choosing them all.

Let me instead trust these friends to know how I appreciate their confidence, their patience, and their impatience. Perhaps especially I needed the last.

Two must be named, however, because my debt there is so specific and so great. In different ways but equally generous, Jane Richtmyer and David Hawkins have understood and loved these six children and hence could help me communicate what I observed and believed to be true about the mornings with them. Having sustained me by the delight they took in the project and the narration of it, they will join I know in the thank-you to those who are my chief support, the six children.

Contents

Preface to the Revised Edition

□■□■□■□■□■□■□■□■□■□■□■□■□■□■□■□■□■

This teacher's notebook, with its story from the lives of six young children, has made its way for some five years to a receptive and responsive audience. For obvious human reasons the response has been gratifying. It has also been humbling and I ask myself why *this* is so. In my years of teaching I have found children's logic and developing reason to be the prime movers in their early learning. My thought when first planning and writing about this particular experience was to communicate something of how those prime movers were discovered, defined, and supported by this individual. I wrote for friends and associates, not hoping for more. But what I have found is a much bigger loyal opposition to standard practice—larger than I had supposed. They stand together, they seek allies and help, but in the meantime they work against narrow ideas of learning for themselves and for children and the narrow practices which follow such ideas.

Among the responses I have gotten are those which

ask for amplification of central theoretical positions. Joseph Featherstone touched on this matter in his very perceptive and early review of *The Logic of Action* in the *New Republic** when he said, "A philosophy of education is here struggling to be heard." He also understood that only many more such personal firsthand accounts will suffice "to articulate it realistically, without dogma or cant."

And so—the changes I have made in the actual text are minor, the additions brief. They are meant only to clarify the account where my terseness had underestimated the impact of brief episodes, episodes which can be seen as paradigms of children at work in appropriate settings.

I have again been brief, believing that in such a notebook the story remains the thing and theory is more to be pursued than expounded ready-made.

There is, however, a theory-pursuing analogy which has long haunted me, and I shall set it forth here. About twenty-five years ago in our dining room I had a discussion with a friend, Dr. Harry Gordon, who was then working with premature babies—premies as they were called—in our medical school's department of pediatrics. He was telling me of the high incidence of blindness among the babies being saved in incubators. In my lay ignorance and audacity I asked whether perhaps the same percentage would have been blind before, had they been saved. I remember his thoughtful answer: "*No*, Frances, we are doing it to them; we are doing something, the *hospital* is doing it."

I remember also the initial profound excitement and shock those words caused in my thirty-five-year-old mind. The excitement I attribute to the realization that I was being spoken to from a frontier. I already knew my informant as a top pediatrician, scientist, friend, and I felt the

* Joseph Featherstone, "The Real Thing in Teaching," *The New Republic*, September 27, 1969, pp. 23–25.

surety of his response reflected knowledge and work to be trusted. I still feel the strength that such men and women in teams around the world can give all of us—all who search.

As some of you will remember and others will have read, this particular mystery—of blindness in premature babies or retrolental fibroplasia—was cracked not long after this episode. This is not the place to go into the details of many clinical and pathological observations from Zacharias to Lelong that led to the final solution, but I would like to quote from a paper by Dr. Theodore Ingalls* so that we may think about the implications of this analogy for our own work with young children and their beginning understanding.

Two other pieces complete the picture and reveal the whole pattern. Many years ago, around nineteen hundred, an Italian anatomist named Riccardo Versari observed that it is during the fifth, sixth and seventh months that a human fetus develops the tiny blood vessels which will nourish the delicate retinas of its eyes. This means that a baby born in those months, ahead of its time, enters the world in a vulnerable condition from the standpoint of its future vision. Any injury which nips these tender shoots, which destroys the growing capillaries, will ultimately manifest its effect in blindness. And so we come at last to the final piece in the "very remarkable chain." Retrolental fibroplasia emerged in epidemic proportions when hospitals began to expose premature babies to very high oxygen atmosphere in efficient new incubators. Often the atmosphere used was more than 50% oxygen (contrasted with 21% in ordinary air).

As Becker-Freyseng succinctly put it: a too rich oxygen atmosphere "acts simultaneously as a *poison* and as a *therapeutic agent.*" The italics are his, but we can adopt them

* "The Strange Case of the Blind Babies," *Scientific American,* December, 1955, pp. 40–44.

as well, for these few words tersely summarize the explanation of the tragedy of oxygen and the sightless babies.

Faced with the failure of children in our schools, their
failure to learn well along the track which school has
paved for them, where are the school doctors (not from
the outside) who will say, with such informed and persistent conviction, "It is something *we* are doing to them,
our schools are doing to them?" Instead of seeing a
child's failure as a response to our doing, to *our* failure, it
becomes a "learning disability," a "behavior problem,"
and we are exonerated.

Very much of what children need for their learning
must come directly and indirectly from adults. As oxygen
to the lungs, it must be readied for them and transmitted
to them. Faced with failure in the process we respond too
easily by increasing the intensity of the efforts which
have already failed, and in doing so we may block the
very channels through which children can gain knowledge and understanding.

High oxygen pressure attacks the delicate lung tissues
of the premature and so decreases the surface area
through which it can be taken into the blood stream. And
so in many of our schools. The input we offer is needed,
yet not assimilated. What we offer with one intent, but
unanalyzed in its total meaning, has signaled another
meaning: *Don't* use your reason, just memorize and pass a
test which will not ask you to think.

I should not be understood as opposing incubators for
the prematures, or "methods" for the teaching of the
young. In every ongoing work, even in the care and education of children, there is a need for elements of mecha-
nization and routine. But these are always a danger. They
cannot be substitutes for learning to observe, for interpreting feedback, for bringing our own reason to bear

upon the challenge of how to educate outside the home.

As the action begins and continues with these six children it is easy to miss—as in the live situation— what these children enact for our instruction and our pleasure. Watch Janie in the midst of a morning—a morning for building—select out the small hinges for special consideration. Their curious attribute, for her—that of opening only part way, was not only carefully explored but also had to be communicated, without words, to friend Patty.

I ask myself as I reread about the quiet and intent Philip. What inner governor gives him such skill and curiosity with materials and phenomena of the world? To provide well for such a child does not imply we understand him; it is the *what* that counts, not the *why*. And that is a blessing.

As you read about Brooke in Visit 6, a morning in which she decides to try her lips, ask yourself to construct something of what must be pushing through in that mind to elicit such a happy sequence of events.

By such playful but serious musings may we increase our understanding of these children, of how it goes (to use a phrase of my friend and colleague Elwyn Richardson) in the Early World.

F.P.H.

March, 1974

There is, then, no difference in kind between verbal
logic and the logic inherent in the co-ordination of actions, but the logic of actions lies deeper down and is
more primitive; it develops more quickly and over-
comes more rapidly the difficulties it meets, but they
are the same difficulties . . . as those that make their
appearance later on the verbal plane.

—Jean Piaget
Studies in Education: First Years in School

Preface, 1969

There are six stories recorded in these pages, but they
rely on translation from the originals—which were told in
the language of action. To the infant of our species this is
a universal language. But for these particular four-year-
olds it was still their only means of communicating; they
are deaf. Through the misfortune of deafness rather than
by design, therefore, we have before us for study some
matters of learning and communication which involve
only the language of action. Of necessity these are heavier
with logic and richer than studies assisted and diluted by
the speech of children who hear.

Among those who hear, beginning in their earliest
days, the universal language of action is interwoven with
the second language, which is spoken. From reliance on
the second language most of us have lost our ability to
enact or to easily comprehend the first. But not all of us
have lost it, and none beyond recovery. Marcel Marceau
creates poetry for us with no words. For a physicist friend

of mine, Philip Morrison, watching that mime's enactment of a man climbing up five flights of stairs with his arms full was a short treatise on the physics of human motion: of balance, of muscle action, of momentum transferred and energy spent.

Some of us must keep and add to our understanding of the early action-language for more practical, though not less interesting, reasons. The loss of it is in turn a kind of deafness, an adult disability in work with all children, but an obvious and absolute loss in work with children in preschool or first grade, who vary so in their ability to speak. This ability cannot be equated with competence of mind. The two are related but there are some nice exceptions to the fashionable belief that they are the same.

I speak of the language of action in this book for another reason: because it is also, and almost synonymously, the language of choice. We choose as we act, we act as we choose. The account of these six children is one of manifold encounters with a planned but unprogrammed environment, and of their choices within it. The restrictions which circumstances put on us affected planning and the range of materials we could bring and are described in the days reported here. These notes and observations illustrate, and perhaps help to elaborate, an essential principle of learning: that given a rich environment—with open-ended "raw" materials—children can be encouraged and trusted to take a large part in the design of their own learning, and that with this encouragement and trust they can learn well. But this is not to be interpreted as advocating a laissez-faire policy. That is easy and very wrong.

From my own years of work with children (from ages three to about nine) I have found that this principle of choice has a far wider and more massive support than the present study provides. Yet I do not underestimate the contribution these six deaf children—in less than two score hours—have made to my understanding and the extension of it. The quality of time cannot be measured by the clock's hands. Who among us—teacher, poet, analyst, lover, physicist, or child damming a stream of water in gutter or gully—does not understand something of time's perversity? The history of these six is very intense in places, then slow and almost becalmed in-between. Work with children that reflects their tempo is often this way. But through these mornings the richness of our non-verbal communication had to be the touchstone, which makes the rhythm more conspicuous, and more demanding of an informed interpretation.

Not only those who teach are concerned with the way in which learning is coupled to choice, active choice. Philosophers, psychologists, and psychotherapists bring special insights which those of us in schools can use. Their different insights remind us that such *visible* aspects of action-language—here the act of choice—are but island tips of the deeper structure we call reason. But it is the teacher who must provide the material from which choices are to be made in a classroom. Later, when a child is less dependent upon his immediate environment for learning, he can better survive a narrow classroom, though why he should have to is another issue.

For me, then, in work with the youngest in school, it is the children themselves who have taught me so much about the principle of choice—exemplified tentative theories, criticized them, suggested, and suffered. More than twenty-five years ago my own apprenticeship began in San Francisco, first in a middle-class district but then for four years in the slums. And there, with depression children and dustbowl refugees, I lost one blind spot—my middle-class "inner eye," * as Ralph Ellison calls that

---

* "That invisibility to which I refer occurs because of a peculiar disposition of the eyes of those with whom I come in contact. A matter of the construction of their *inner* eyes, those eyes with which they look

mechanism which interferes with seeing reality. I began
to see these children as strong and hungry to learn. The
school administration tried in more than one way to convince me that such children could not really learn very
much. But I was too naïve and stubborn to be persuaded
of that establishment tenet, and the children and their
parents supported me with much contrary evidence.
Together we were willing to render unto Caesar: by quiet
behavior in halls and, when necessary, in class. So we
were left alone though given no encouragement.

After teaching in nursery and elementary schools in
various places and situations I recently returned to my
first loves in the slums of a large eastern city. I found
them there, with their inquisitive minds, inventive hands,
with their strengths and weaknesses, and I knew that after
having been too long in the public schools their strengths
would become invisible and their weaknesses empha-
sized. That is what happens except in rare cases.

In another book I hope to analyze and illustrate from
work with other children how they have helped me to
shape many facets of the learning theories I trust as
guides. But the present story has a special place in the
formulation of my ideas about language and learning.
The misfortune of deafness brings into high relief the significance and the role of the language of action, when
that language must, for so long, remain the only means of
communication, when it must indicate subtleties and
depths designed for the spoken language. Both of these
languages—of action and of speaking—depend upon and
are interlocked with the underlying logic and reason.

---

through their physical eyes upon reality. . . . You ache with the need
to convince yourself that you do exist in the real world, that you're part
of all the sound and anguish, and you strike out with your fists, you
curse and you swear to make them recognize you. And, alas it's seldom
successful," *Invisible Man*, New York: Random House, 1947, p. 3.

Introduction

□■□■□■□■□■□■□■□■□■□■□■□■□■□■□■□■□■

THE SCHOOL

The setting of our story is Fillmore Elementary School, as
I shall call it. It is located in an inner city within commut-
ing distance from my home. The area around Fillmore is
quietly blighted. Slums take time to mature, and in some
of our newer western cities "blight" is often the more
appropriate word, unless the rate of decay has been unusually high or the beginnings unusually shabby. The Watts
of my childhood, in the booming Los Angeles of the twen-
ties, was already then a slum. (We knew it and as adoles-
cents made jokes about it. With shame one remembers.)
The Fillmore district is not yet Watts.

The Fillmore building itself is of sturdy brick construction which was prized at the turn of the century, and
not without reason. The halls are wide, ceilings high, and
the classrooms are spacious and well lighted by their
many windows along one side, almost low enough for
small children to see out. What the playground was like
for the children of sixty years ago I do not know. Now it is
sterile—paved, securely fenced, and unimaginatively pro-
visioned in a minimal standard way.

Along the side of the playground and into the enor-
mous hall of Fillmore I walked that first morning, memory
my companion. Floor oil saturated the worn wood and

damped my foot sounds just as it was supposed to do. Whoever has known it cannot forget the smell. I knew that behind each closed door were living beings and I still do not understand, after living and working in schools both old like this and shiny new, why they contrive to erase any evidence of life within. The silence, the bulletin boards hung with children's neat best efforts, the aura of authority unseen—these things told me that little had changed since my early years of teaching in just such a school, a thousand miles away in space and thirty years in time.

THE CHILDREN

I came to the room I was seeking and went in. But before that narrowing of my story, there are useful impressions to relate gained from later visits to Fillmore. About half the children whose school this is come from the surrounding streets. They tiptoe through the halls and appear to be subdued and frightened, especially the younger ones. On the playground they are bored and aggressive, especially the older ones. They are poorly nourished; they wear faded hand-me-downs or poignantly new party clothes; and the striking disadvantage of poverty overshadows racial differences of their Spanish, Mexican, Anglo, or African origins. They are all Americans.

Deaf or hard-of-hearing children make up the remaining enrollment, and those of them who do not live in the neighborhood are brought to Fillmore by bus. Our nursery school group was delivered at 7:30 and picked up at 10:30. All the bused deaf children come from a wider segment of the population, the middle class, and reflect in the greater homogeneity of their racial background the Anglo-American predominance outside the inner city. This, too, is American.

We have here a mixture of handicaps—of poverty and of physical deprivation. It is a delicate expedient, but by no means an unpromising one, to combine two such groups. Here at Fillmore, however, poor children were treated (and, one suspects, punished) as if unhandicapped, and the hard-of-hearing were treated narrowly for that handicap. Troubles are quickly compounded when both of these groups are in need of enrichment that neither is getting, though each could help provide it for the other with a bit of careful planning. The aggressive behavior we saw in the playground reflected a relationship between children which gave little reassurance about what was going on in the classrooms.

OUR PLACE AND ROLE IN THE CLASSROOM *

The group of four-year-olds we came to work with had a new and special standing in this public school. Their teacher, Miss M., was working under a university-sponsored program called Language Arts,† and was not employed by the public school, although it provided the space and basic equipment (including toys and accoustical devices). I had been asked by the professor in charge of the Language Arts program to participate in it, to bring variety and enrichment from my experience with children of this age using materials of early science. We worked out a pattern with all concerned of giving one morning a week to this, a fifth of the children's time in school, for some fifteen weeks.

A curious and unplanned circumstance had the effect of isolating our one morning a week with the children.

* Claire Grusin joined me as photographer and secretary at the third visit. She was a recent graduate in political science who came to our Science Advisory Center as a secretary. Occasional visitors to our small center would visit Fillmore School with me and be put to work.

† See the résumé of this program, in Appendix 1.

Our early visits with Miss M. were pleasant and, in terms of my personal relationship with her, continued to be easy. But I soon realized that in welcoming our efforts she lived comfortably with the conviction that what we brought had no connection with her Language Arts. I had hoped that some liveliness in what we did would inevitably weave its way into her days and enrich them. But these notes will show something of how Miss M. and I developed and kept to our roles since I had been asked to work with the children and not with the young teacher. If Miss M. sensed any relationship between our visits and her own work, she kept it to herself until the very end of the term.

In the years since I was at Fillmore, I have worked primarily with teachers. These years keep open for me the key question in such advisory work: Can any adult make use of help he has *not* requested? I think the answer is no—others will disagree. Here it should be remembered that Miss M. had not asked for help. She welcomed us as co-workers, and though I tried to stay in that role, I was only partially successful.

How did the children themselves react to what seemed to me, in this dichotomy of understandings, a threat to our usefulness? They made out of it the best of two worlds, and took grist for their mills from each. They navigated with a sure touch and generous insight. They folded away their once-a-week behavior and interests with us on their days with Miss M., and to some extent they held in reserve their attitudes toward Miss M.'s work while with us. The absence of language underlined the separation here, as it does the separation of other parts of these children's lives.

Still another factor contributed to the isolation of our work. In the beginning we left some of our materials at the school between visits, but Miss M. indicated to us that this complicated her language work with the children. Until the end of the term, therefore, when Miss M. requested some of the equipment, nothing remained between visits.

In spite of their encapsulation, however, our visits were not without effect on Miss M. and there is some evidence of twoway carry-over in these notes. Because she genuinely liked the children, Miss M. enjoyed the evidence of their development and hence generously acknowledged it when she saw that it was furthered by our visits. I am convinced, however, that she did not—was not ready to—understand how and why the children themselves used our mornings for their growth. (To see evidence of a parent's understanding, see page 73.) I have included in the notes some remarks which indicate Miss M.'s appreciation. In return we encouraged her, I believe, to rely on her own better inclinations, which the school establishment did not do.

EVALUATION

Each student of these pages will have to decide whether and where we inadvertently credit to our Thursdays growth which cannot be so pinpointed. The continuation of our visits depended on my judgment as to whether or not our work accelerated and heightened the children's development.

The prime uncertainty in our evaluations is related, of course, to a possible underestimation of the children's powers of growth in the absence of what we brought to involve them and to encourage diversification. To watch this group is to be struck again by the variety of learning patterns, of curiosities still intact, of degrees of self-guidance. It is to be reminded of how unequally very young children take school—almost any school—in stride and learn from it.

Any school values its effectiveness too highly if it measures itself by the achievements of those already well on their way. It may then in reality only be standing still and maintaining the status quo—not enough by far for man's survival. Especially in these days when ghettos are bursting out from narrow restrictions, school can and must matter more than that. In assessing our report, readers should look especially for evidence of the transitions they would judge unlikely for *this* child in a *more conventional* environment. Did these mornings of work with simple materials of early science count for these deaf children beyond what each, with his own given powers and deficiencies, could have gained without us?

In defense of the judgments I made—my assistant was a beginner and followed my lead—there is one factor to be mentioned. Such young children stand close to many beginnings. Because these early years are rich with fresh shoots it is more likely than with older children that we see change and effect it, not merely infer change from unknown sources. Here lies the excitement of designing for and working with the very young. Here too the danger of overestimating one's influence *or* of designing too precisely—too explicitly.

The careful recording of observation is already a step removed from the action itself. This step is a much shorter and more reliable one, I believe, than those often taken for the sake of achieving one-dimensional ranking and numerical measure. For then the onus is very clearly upon the evaluator to show that in mapping the plenitude of a child's career upon a few linear standard scales, he is indeed filtering out the germ and not a handful of chaff. In the redundancy of a narrative with many interlocking observations there is a crosschecking of states and changes of state which can achieve a statistical reliability far greater than what we get from the reduction of a few preselected data, however obtained. Statistical theory testifies to this conclusion, though it gives us no magic formulas into which to plug the information we have relied upon here.

THE PHOTOGRAPHS AND THEIR USE FOR THE CHILDREN

It has been a help to us, and may assist the reader, to have in the photographs an independent record. They give pictorial definition to what we valued so heavily as a positive indication of growth—the deep and sequential involvement of the children in their work. To Claire Grusin we owe great gratitude for these photographs.

Illustrating these notes are facsimiles of Claire's pictures which were originally arranged as notebook pages and sent home with each child when we had a page or two ready. Only after some weeks with the children had I realized that we could use these pictures as a bridge, in their world of deafness, between school and home. From the beginning we were involved in the difficulty of communication except in terms of here and now. Recall, reference to absent family or other matters, required such imagination as to make the effort almost too difficult for all of us. These being young humans, the need to remember and discuss was great, and in these notes the reader will be struck by how often the children indicated their need.*

Once the decision was made to send the pictures home, the next step was obvious: to include the children's budding reading abilities with the pictures. And so sentences which were based on but not identical with their knowledge of the printed word were added. The chil-

* See Lisa noticing Claire's burn in Visit 6 (p. 62).

dren's reactions to the first pages they saw are described
in Visit 8.

There is a small but sturdy band of teachers, some already in the field and most just entering, who have asked
in one way or another that these notes include my own
understanding, beliefs, and mode of operating. "Please
don't put it down as if it just magically happens for *you*,"
young Karen Weisskopf Worth once requested, thus helping me to clarify a need. I have tried to meet that request
by taking off from a particular incident where the children
spell out *for me* the reality of my theoretical understanding of how learning occurs, contradict it, or, what is
even more to the point, add to and change that understanding.

"Explain why you decided to . . ." other friends ask.
And so I have included some of those tangents to my
planning and analysis which I think are adjacent to the
circle of action. I am deeply grateful for these requests,
which gave me courage to elaborate and write down what
must remain a personal kind of thinking. Contrary to the
thoughtful reaction of a good critic, I find that the result-
ing unevenness of these notes is not unlifelike and hope
that teachers of the young will agree.

My associates, here and abroad, defined well what
they asked for. My own failures in complying must not be
in any sense their responsibility.

About the Six Children

□■□■□■□■□■□■□■□■□■□■□■□■□■□■□■□■□■□■□■

Just how much and what a teacher should know in advance about the children in her class is a matter of disagreement in the field. I prefer to be told little, to be forced to observe much. Far from implying that I do not value a child's out-of-school life, this preference means that I do not trust the effect of an information filter of the sort created by others' observations and evaluations on my own early analysis.

What concerns me as a teacher is the child's behavior as it reflects his anxieties and joys; his physical posture, energy, and health; his choices and refusals; his habits and humor. To get so wide a picture of a child outside his home requires a classroom rich in challenge and variety with a climate of probing, trying, weighing. If this cumulative information proves inadequate for me to provide well for a child, *then* I must seek help from a parent, a social worker, or a therapist. In this spirit, then, let me provide only brief preliminary information.

These six children test as "profoundly deaf." They wear the hearing aids one sees in the pictures on the plausible theory that any kind of sound heard is stimulating and useful. But I have been told that among those who work with the deaf there is disagreement about what is gained, for children *as deaf as these*, by using the aids.

Having watched these children I can understand why there is disagreement. I was able to see no effect. That does not say there was none. Occasionally an ear plug would start a screaming oscillation and Miss M. would go over and turn it down. Though audible across the room, the children apparently heard nothing of the shrill sounds. The cause of deafness in these children varied. For some it was congenital and for others it was from early illness.

When we started our work with them the children's ages were:

LISA 4 years, 1 month   PHILLIP 4 years, 2 months

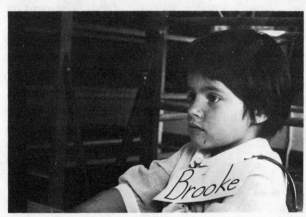

BROOKE
4 years, 9 months

The Cast

JANIE 4 years, 8 months

PATTY 3 years, 10 months

GREG 4 years, 2 months

It is obvious that psychoanalysts, who deal mainly with the verbal communications of the adult, will have to undertake a more systematic study of the earliest, archaic forms of communication in infancy if they want to arrive at an understanding of adult communication on one hand, and the beginnings of thought process on the other. In view of the fact that the genetic aspects of psychoanalysis are stressed so consistently, it is surprising that such a study has not been undertaken long ago.

—Rene A. Spitz
No and Yes: On the Genesis of Human Communication

Observation, Please

□■□■■□■□■□■□■□■□■□■□■□■□■□■□■□■□■□■□■

VISIT 1, JANUARY 19

When an old hand steps into a young teacher's classroom as an observer, it is not clear who, in the net of human beings caught there, is most nervous. A formal class for the young in the United States is particularly formidable because it is so quiet, programmed, and dominated by its teacher, and at such variance with a young child's patterns of life. It was nevertheless a surprise, since I am an incurable optimist, that on this first morning at Fillmore with deaf four-year-olds I found a formal group-reading lesson going on.

The walk by the yard and through the long hall had chilled me. The long time it took for Miss M., the children, and me to become communicating human beings, even on a surface level, is a more specific commentary on the operation of our schools. (In Africa, England, and even in France I have found less apprehension.)

I sat down quickly at the back of the reading group and swallowed my own trepidation. I reminded myself not to react to the establishment, with its continuing unawareness of children's natures and needs. I had been invited, first of all, to observe and I behaved—for a while.

I watched the attractive young teacher working with her six children from 8:30 to 9:00. The lesson was standard for a kind of roll taking: cut-up sentences were to be put together in slots at the reading board to read LISA IS HERE, GREG IS HERE, MRS. MARTIN IS NOT HERE. This procedure was sensible and useful as a morning's opener as long as it made sense to those who were in fact *here*, and was not prolonged into drill separated from reality. That morning the children's involvement varied from Brooke's deep interest to Phillip's total withdrawal of anything that could conceivably be labeled attention. Greg's face and manner were unresponsive, and he glanced often toward me, the intruder.

Since none of these children spoke a word, Miss M.'s was the only voice. She selected a child to carry a name to the board and fit it to the correct incomplete sentence. To communicate her selection she touched the child or spoke his name if he was watching her face and could lip-read a bit. Apart from special problems of communication and the more crucial need of these deaf children, the atmosphere and the answer-pulling (in this case action-pulling) were familiar for this type of silent group-reading with hearing children. (See page 58 for evidence of Brooke's understanding and reading.)

The children had come at 7:30, had been sitting a long time, and were getting restless. Miss M. was understandably nervous, and spoke to me in asides: "He can't sit still . . . He's been out for ten days and can't remember a thing." I was unable to stand up and make a sensible move such as saying, "Darlings—the seven of you—let's stop this. Enough is enough!" The 9:00 break for milk and coffee rescued us all and we walked down the hall to the cafeteria. Lock step was about to be broken.

I could see that Miss M. was fond of these children. I realized only later that a handicap in this setting was her lack of experience with the very young. She was interested in the university-sponsored program, but having worked previously with the age range from nine to twenty-one, she could not yet appreciate how to accommodate or apply what she knew to these beginners.

In the large, bare cafeteria that first morning we all sat at the adult-size table, smallest chins at table level. Miss M. brought a tray from the kitchen with individual milk cartons, straws, and graham crackers for the children. The tray was pushed by the children, in a perfunctory manner, from one to another. There was some silent signaling among them. For example, one would break crackers in a way-to-be-copied, as hearing threes and fours do. The others would copy and then, looking at each other, would eat the crackers to the last crumb. The tray was again pushed from child to child and empty cartons put on it. The routine had been maintained. The adults had coffee and cookies, and *this* adult was not learning enough about the children.

To stimulate some spontaneous (and hence more significant) behavior, I broke routine and put my coffee cup on the children's tray. (Miss M. had politely indicated that our cups should be carried to the kitchen.) Astonishment was the immediate reaction on the children's faces as they looked from each other to my out-of-place cup. Then they expressed this astonishment to one another by pointing as if to say, "Look what that grownup did!" Their change of facial expression encouraged me. I joined their reaction in mock censure of myself and the joke was shared by some.

Two or three children cautioned me that I was *not* to do that by shaking heads and fingers at me—with humor—as children do with relish when pleasant conspiracy beckons.

Feeling that I had succeeded in some sort of exchange with the children I continued. To an accompaniment of louder, strange throat-laughter (the first I'd heard), I next turned the coffee cup upside down on the tray. Now the laughter turned to apprehensive glances at Miss M.—I had gone too far! Miss M. laughed, with relief I thought, at the way I was failing to fit the school pattern, at my obvious lack of respect for unwritten law. The children, in turn, took their cue from Miss M. and apprehension became curiosity, a more useful-by-product for school. We had established our first channel of rapport, shared over forbidden fruit.

When we returned to the classroom Miss M. asked me to try some sort of game with the children. Since I had already entered the arena—if only with nonsense—she was justified in turning to me, and so I tried an old hand-and-finger game, "Open, shut them," with the children sitting around me on the floor. It was obvious at once that though they understood, there was minimal interest, and I was pleased that they could indicate this by walking away. It spoke well of the relationship between children and teacher that they were not afraid. It more strongly indicated, I realized later, their awareness of routine: this was playtime.

I asked whether, instead, I could watch the children at play with the equipment in their room (good blocks, trucks, doll buggies, and jungle gym which had been donated by one of the women's organizations interested in preschools for the deaf). My implied belief that the children and I could learn from free play was a welcome but improbable idea for Miss M. "Most people think nothing of importance goes on in free play," she said. Now I was

permitted to see these children in a situation where they
were all actively choosing and structuring for themselves.

This free time, Miss M. later confessed to my appreciative ears, she had clandestinely allowed the children to
have, each day, as part of their three-hour morning. She
volunteered, in addition, that when the children had first
come they didn't play well together. This comment was in
response to my praise for their sense of unity and self-
direction as a group. This was honest praise which I was
happy and relieved to be able to give.

During this morning I occasionally joined the children's play which, *if silence can be ignored,* was normal
to their age and milieu. Not a word was used spontane-
ously. At the teacher's request, however, two of the children as they left laboriously mimicked "bye-bye" in the
monotone of early deaf speech. Miss M. held their arms
so that they would watch her mouth. Some weeks later
one of Lisa's younger brothers came with his mother to
take her home. While he was on the jungle gym he called
out, "Hey Mom, look!" I was startled. Hearing a child's
voice made me suddenly aware of how we had accepted
the unnatural silence.

By late morning Miss M. and I were at ease with each
other and her understandable suspicion of me, as presum-
ably just another member of the school establishment,
was gone. In my own mind I was searching for ways in
which I might be useful.

It is my primary concern to understand, identify, and
help to change what is wrong with out schools for the
young, especially in the inner cities, so that children can
learn. Unless I could work here to further that end, I
thought I could not afford the time and would withdraw.
But as I watched these children using their minds at play,
communicating with no spoken language, I realized that
this was a unique opportunity. For me, a student of early
learning, the language of action *and its logic* would be

thrown into high relief by the pervasive silence of these lives. In retrospect, I know that with this realization the die was already cast.

To provide myself with more evidence, I interfered again. The interruption was minimal and had to do with introducing into the arena of three children who were building with blocks a large cardboard box which was used to store the blocks. I tipped it on its side and moved a small truck into it, thinking of a garage. The children's reaction to this investment of an empty box with possibilities for use was indicative of their response to any novelty or variation suggested by an adult. They were amazed at my entrance.

There was, I should underline, a totally passive attitude on the part of Miss M. toward the play period. This was in direct contrast to her kindly-authoritarian, sometimes annoyed, attitude during "Language Arts." In their programming for young children, neophytes commonly see their role as either/or: either completely in control or completely withdrawn. It takes time and experience to find a more natural way of stepping in and out, and Miss M.'s experience, with older children only, complicated her learning of this delicate timing with young deaf children. Although that kind of detail cannot be laid out in advance, it can be nourished by apprenticeship with an experienced and thoughtful teacher.

But watch the children. When I tipped the large cardboard box on its side, the three builders looked at me with surprised scrutiny. I cannot quite interpret their meaning but it seemed to question: my role? whether the box was a plaything? what their response should be? Then with a consensus of action they turned the box back on its bottom and showed me a thing or two.

For many minutes they played. Three could fit inside the box scrunched together . . . They climbed in and out, one two or three . . . They closed the flaps . . . One sat on top . . . They knocked on the closed box, with one inside and two out. On and on and on, oblivious of observers, they invented as they played. The unspoken excitement and exploitation of the box showed me these children internalizing bits and pieces of relational ideas: *inside, outside, closed, open, empty, full.* I mused on how one would use such involvement to build these words into reading and speaking at an appropriate later time. I was challenged. I wished for deeper involvement. At such a moment an observer—teacher, therapist, or diagnostician—prays for time for the children at engrossed play; for herself to remain a relatively unnoticed member of the scene.

Later in the morning one of the children felt my purse, in a way common to some younger, hearing children, which reminded me that I had in it a small flashlight-magnifier. I took it out and showed how the light turned on, how one could look through the eyepiece. Everyone had a turn of some sort, and so did I. Some children wanted to try again. Brooke had a turn and seemed to see something through it, but I wasn't sure; she certainly tried it with understanding. Lisa's behavior was so obvious that one could understand it. She went through all the motions she had observed me making, but they were totally divorced from any reason for doing them (e.g., she bent toward the eyepiece but did not look). This, of course, is not uncommon behavior in a baby who mimics what he cannot yet understand. It is useful information about Lisa because it suggests that she is used to observing, but primarily in order to mimic—since she is not reaching the reasons behind observed action. This must be a relatively common lag with deaf children.

Watching the others with the magnifier, I felt that while they could not yet use it well, they saw that something was changed in what they glimpsed. Greg, for example, gave it back quickly when he realized that he didn't understand. This was a useful insight into *his* pattern of approaching something new—embarrassment. He will be one of the self-timers. Lisa's pattern, on the other hand, asked for help. It is instructive to follow the later development of these children as they explored more materials that are understood by use.

After school Miss M. and I discussed the episode of the box: how it was obvious that implicit information about *empty, full, three*, etc., was being put into place *for* these children *by* them, and that appropriate explicit words could follow in reading and speaking, the more easily if one remembered and used such rootlets and provided others. From this and later conversations with Miss M. I assumed more than I should have about her understanding of the close coupling between the thing and the naming of it. I realize now that a concurrent seminar was needed, but circumstances on both sides seemed to make this impossible.

TO CONSIDER:

1. I want to note a bit more about my early analysis of this group of children in the setting of free play and routine—against a background of the behavior of hearing children of the same age and economic circumstance. The children's reliance on routine and their awareness of any variation from that routine, even in play, was much greater than with most four-year-olds, though this age can easily become a conforming one for any children when maintained in too narrow a setting. These children, I observed, used too little initiative with materials provided by the teacher in lessons or directions; they too closely watched for a routine to follow. In this again they are not unlike older schoolchildren in bleak settings and more dictatorial atmospheres, who rely less and less on the inner and often competent direction they bring from

home. In such atmospheres it is as if the open or disguised denigration of who they are and what they bring from economically poor or culturally different homes finally destroys or transforms to violence what it has failed to honor. Writers such as O'Casey and Gorky speak with clarity about that piece of truth.* We see it happen to our children in class after class, with monotonous certainty.

2. What is sometimes rudeness and often ignorance on the part of adults, namely, to speak about children rather than to them, to laugh at them rather than with them, is easy to fall into with deaf children. I must avoid it, I cautioned myself. For them, genuine understanding, beyond following orders, *and* two-way communication are difficult enough. We are all guilty of surface communication. A question: Could the bad habit of talking about older deaf children and adults in their presence contribute to their paranoid troubles?

3. When a habitual occurrence like mealtime is treated in too routine and mechanical a fashion, possibilities are bypassed. Shouldn't the eating period for these children, where communication is limited, be a time for varied experience? Cartons of milk could be carried to a corner of their own room, or the question posed, "Where shall we eat this morning? Yesterday we had our milk under the jungle gym." The necessary repetition of eating can always be a theme for variations, the same props enhanced and valued by change in the setting. My deliberate small interruptions of routine evoked first a surprise that implied dependency. Increasing independence will follow when children welcome and then invent such novelties as the stuff of learning—of good living.

* Sean O'Casey, *I Knock at the Door;* Maxim Gorky, *My Childhood.*

In man's brain the impressions from the outside are not merely registered; they produce concepts and ideas. They are the imprint of the external world upon the human brain. Therefore, it is not surprising that, after a long period of searching and erring, some of the concepts and ideas in human thinking should have come gradually closer to the fundamental laws of this world.

—Victor F. Weisskopf
Knowledge and Wonder: The Natural World As Man Knows It

On Planning— to Learn

□ ■ □ ■ □ ■ □ ■ □ ■ □ ■ □ ■ □ ■ □ ■ □ ■ □ ■ □ ■ □ ■ □ ■ □ ■ □ ■ □ ■

VISIT 2, JANUARY 27

Equipment *

hamster in cage

straws, cans, and soap mixture for blowing bubbles

tire tube and air pump

large plastic syringes for air and water play

transparent plastic tubes (about 3 feet long, 1 inch diameter) filled with colored water, corked and sealed

* See Appendix 2 for a fuller description of equipment listed throughout. Since the classroom was barren of what I would call usable junk, we brought supplies of newspapers, rags, cans, etc. to back up and make usable our more "scientific" equipment. The junk is obvious and will not be listed each time. In a proper classroom it would naturally be provided.

This morning's equipment list reflects something of my thinking during the two weeks since the first visit. I have mentioned the apparent contrast between the children's approach to "school affairs" and their approach to "free play." While there were individual differences in their reactions to Miss M.'s reading games, these were differences within the grooved spirit of rote, and contrasted startlingly with their liveliness in free play. Anyone who has taken the time to notice, has made similar observations of hearing children. In some very poignant sense, of course, these children are more at our mercy than hearing children are. Their deaf ears have denied them a potential source of variation and novelty—though with many a hearing child such dry, repetitive lessons are equally out of joint.

In planning for this first working, but still essentially diagnostic, morning, therefore, I wanted to increase the input. I asked myself how best to tap the children's *existing* energies and innovative powers for using beginning language, and how to find new concepts for their wider learning, separate from words but readied for verbal expression. That was the general aim. In designing the morning I was especially conscious of two sorts of conditions that are always necessary in competent teaching.

In the Preface I speak of the principle of choice as it contributes to learning when there is richness in the environment and children are using well their innate capacities for choice. The first condition is met by providing appropriate materials which they can use or transform, from which to make choices. This being school, there is a corollary about teachers' choices and teachers' learning. In order to learn about the children a teacher must choose at two levels: first, in the selection of materials to be provided and then, more subtly, at the level of teaching. A teacher can make choices as to whether, when, and how to intervene in the learning process when it is not going well and when it is going very well indeed. Thus, to meet the second condition a teacher must *plan to learn* about the children through *their* choices and so begin to acquire specific content and definition, from each child, for the variables of *significant* choice and quality of involvement. In turn, it is only through such learning—learning how a child is building between his own deeply hidden reason or understanding and what we *see* him *do*—that a teacher can modify initial goals and materials or intervene successfully to enhance the ongoing process. The ability to expedite learning depends upon how fast and accurately a teacher learns to assess and analyze children's individual patterns, strengths, and needs.

Let me speak first of my own need to know. I had formed some strong impressions about these children and the narrow range of their response to school. But it tempers audacity to enter, as I was doing, a field unfamiliar though closely related to one's own. Accepting gross differences around the fact of deafness, I aimed at the identification of likenesses between these children and their hearing cousins, and then again at the uncovering of differences (over and above individual variations) in their ways of being alike. I needed to test my first conclusions and refine them. *I needed more samplings and soundings from the children themselves, at work, and more thinking about these observations away from the children in order to provide well.*

Both for these reasons of my own and because the narrowed channels for receiving would require from me a greater input planned in greater detail than beginnings usually need to be, I selected carefully from materials whose potentialities I had tested pretty well in the past, and extrapolated from them in certain areas for these six children. Local circumstances also affected the choice—

they usually do. We traveled some distance to the school
and had to carry our materials each time. Any school in-
novator will realize that there was also the problem of
"keeping school property clean and neat." I did not want
to put Miss M. in the position of having to defend our
messy junk or store it; so we brought it and took it back, a
car trunk full each time. This eliminated much—sand, for
example, and growing things.

But now to uncovering children's needs. Careful planning must and can avoid the trap of narrowness. To program learning often means to hamper it by restricting
children to the stereotyped anticipations of the program-
mer. With four- and five-year-olds of normal hearing our
schools tend to do this, to restrict the curriculum or
weight it with puzzles that demand the "right" answer,
with questions that ask the child to guess what is meant,
with activities that fail to invite innovation. There are
times and places for such designing—such puzzles—but
when a room is dominated by predigested material the
message is implicit: others have done the thinking, *you
memorize.*

Not long before my Fillmore experience I had observed a nursery school where bells rang, lights flashed,
M&Ms were dispensed, and other forms of strong praise
exuded to reinforce the right performance in a context
of preset goals and predigested content. So I was particularly on guard and cautioned myself not to straighten and
confine the offering but to broaden it, to build in an initial
multiplicity—and to trip some laughter. The fact that one
tries to provide this multiplicity in teaching "normal"
children only underlined the proposition that here it
would be indispensable.

Such a multiplicity of things to do, things important to
children, can have a kind of thematic unity centered
around related phenomena. This is one way of planning
for the youngest, but it is not lesson planning.

I want to be very clear about this distinction, in view of the loose and conventional use of such words as "structured" and "unstructured," "authoritarian" and "laissez faire." These terms may be useful in specific cases to suggest something measurable on a linear scale, but they only confuse the description of complex settings where learning, not parroting, is the focus for young children. How a child selects and uses material from the initial provisioning depends upon him and upon his unique store of experience. His behavior expresses his present *and developing* resources and concomitantly increases my understanding of how and what to plan with and for him and of how to respond immediately.

The plan is thus a joint and dynamic kind of product, better seen *as* a plan in retrospect than in prospect. But the teacher must assume with care the first responsibility—to select well—so that the child can accept and exercise his own responsibility. It is in this way, in this web of activity, that the two kinds of conditions for good teaching and learning can both be satisfied.

What evolved as my starting point, then, was a loosely patterned morning centered around the related phenomena of water, bubbles, and air. Hamster came as a sort of check, an alternative and contrasting offering. The classroom itself contained the good standard stuff. How things would go thereafter would be determined from the morning's activity, from my assessment of what the children actually made of our provisions. Could they select, design, and take some responsibility? Could they abstract? That was the key question. I thought I knew part of the answer, but I needed to let the children spell it out in their unique ways.

At first they flitted from one to another cluster of the material, which I had arranged on tables. There was little sticking to one thing, much watching to see what the teacher and other children were doing, and hence little

time for experimental use even of bubbles and water. The
sealed plastic tubes were picked up in a cursory manner,
noticed and then put down—with one or two exceptions,
when a child really watched the bubble rise as he tipped
the tube. It was not unlike the Christmas morning syndrome which one can identify for most children in the
opening days of a good school. It was more striking here
because there were fewer children in the class than is
usual for this age, and the contagion of one child's use of
something spread to the others rapidly and more visibly.
But even so, there was little significant choice. Whatever
I did was immediately copied, and, as one must when this
happens I had to change what I started as quickly as possible, provide more than one way to copy, thus sanction-
ing and inviting variety.

This imitative reaction is useful to a teacher as an indication of what a child deems important at the moment—
to copy another child? to copy teacher? to find a *right* answer? (I recall from my first teaching days with too much
lesson planning how many children there were who
learned to copy everything just as I "taught" it. It made
me feel successful, until slowly I began to see the mistakes made by some children as tangents to be encouraged, expanded on, learned from—not always, not
randomly, but often. When a group of fives produces replica upon replica of one paper ornament it is time to
watch for and dignify, perhaps by hanging from a mobile,
one child's "mistake"—one hard to copy and thus con-
ducive to the production of still more "mistakes."

Two weeks before, it will be remembered, the children had used the blocks and other standard equipment
in the room with some freedom and spark of invention.
Early this morning their old school stuff was ignored and
any imagination seemed set aside along with it. Did the
coupling to a new teacher make the children watchful and

wary ("Don't think or test or experiment . . .")? Was there too much variety? Or were we at a beginning which the children felt should be lightly touched, tentatively examined, and thought about?

Hamster slept most of the morning and was something of a loss though we communicated through action about sleeping—ours and his. Perhaps because he usually sleeps in the daytime, Hamster will suggest that living beings cannot be *made* to perform? The nice idea that he was awake when the children slept was too much for me to tackle through pantomime at this early stage.

When the bubbling stuff was mixed and ready, Miss M. said to me (to save Brooke from failure, I felt), "Brooke can't blow." However, since the setup was easy and did not require any particular performance, I gave Brooke, who was reaching for it, a can of suds and a straw—and she *did* make bubbles, even if in a stacatto and unsustained fashion. (It was found out later that parts of Brooke's throat were semiparalyzed.) A blow is a blow, and while the other children could perform in a more sustained way they were by no means adept at blowing, which suggested that they were not used to having the chance. I should have thought that any pleasurable action using mouth and diaphragm would be a must for children who are trying to acquire speech at such a disadvantage.

From the children's manifest unfamiliarity with any of the phenomena, and their suppressed excitement at trying things (even though so briefly at first), I judged them to be hungry for wider and less programmed experience with materials that are open-ended in possibilities for use. While their individual styles of learning and of structuring materials to foster this learning are falling into place, language will be impoverished since it will have to be supplied in an unnatural way. Perhaps by adding a dimension of richness just here I may be useful. Certain of these children can already communicate very simply through written words. For others it is still to come. If the seed of emerging language can be nourished by vital experience with natural phenomena which behave differently (under varied circumstances and/or in response to individual probing), then we will have matters to share, to wonder at, to understand, to write and read about, which will be close to these growing minds.

One may distinguish the mechanics of language for these children from the spontaneous use and enjoyment of it. But to distinguish is not to separate them totally, and I propose to work at the early level where I believe that *not to separate* is particularly important. When the art and skill of using language is marked off and delimited as a special "subject," the powers of an early learner are correspondingly enfeebled. Silence pervades a classroom of the deaf, of course, and a newcomer to it, practiced in sharing and interpreting the talk of young children, is keenly aware of the missing dimensions of their recall and description. These lacks are challenging since one depends upon such talking, especially when getting to know certain children. Fortunately, all fours and fives have their language of action to fall back upon, and so does a teacher.

My reading of today's visit is favorable to the plans I have made, but I look forward to next week for evidence of more sustained and less stereotyped efforts with similar but even more open-ended materials.

Bubbles

Lisa is here.
Patty is here.
Brooke is here.

Janie is here.
Greg is here.
They are blowing bubbles.
Phillip is not here.

Phillip is here.
He is making
bubbles
in the water.

In his everyday life play is the child's natural form of expression, a language that brings him into a communicating relationship with others and with the world in which he lives. Through play he learns the meaning of things and the relation between objects and himself; and in play he provides himself with a medium of motor activity and emotional expression.

—Frederick Harold Allen
Psychotherapy With Children

Many Things to Play With

□ ■ □ ■ □ ■ □ ■ □ ■ □ ■ □ ■ □ ■ □ ■ □ ■ □ ■ □ ■ □ ■ □ ■ □ ■ □ ■

VISIT 3, FEBRUARY 10

Equipment *

large plastic tub to replace individual cans for blowing bubbles
Attribute Blocks
plastic tubes of various lengths and diameters
corks of assorted diameters, to be used by children to make their own closed bubble tubes
plastic funnels
flashlight-magnifier

It was on this visit that Claire Grusin joined me to take photographs and make on-the-spot notes of each session.

When we arrived today the children were drinking

---

* Except as noted, the equipment listed each week is in addition to that previously provided.

milk in the cafeteria. We were greeted with grinning faces, silence, and then with questioning looks at Claire. She was introduced, and Lisa immediately felt her purse, and then mine. The small flashlight-magnifier was still in my purse, remembered from my first visit, and Lisa seemed reassured when she identified it through the soft leather. She grinned at me as she touched it. When this behavior is transfered to Claire is it a substitute for language: "What's your name? Who are you? Do you belong together, you two? Do you carry the same things in your purses? Will you come again?"

Janie's hair had been cut short since I last saw them, and communication about hair cutting took place among some of us. Other children joined the pantomime conversation, each showing how his or her hair had also been cut once upon a time. Their need to remember and to discuss the barbershop is certainly as keen as any hearing child's. They are bursting to talk, to communicate with outsiders like Claire and me, and in the absence of language, their artfulness in asking and telling is indicative of good minds at work.

Miss M. was relaxed, friendly, and obviously pleased to have us there. This attitude encouraged our visits. If she had felt we were intruders, we could not have continued.

While we were still sitting at the lunch table one child noticed and indicated by pointing that I did not have on a name tag. All the children reacted to the observation and communication from the first child. In a matter-of-fact way, with minimal gestures, Miss M. told Brooke to go and get my name tag from the classroom. With speed Brooke returned, MRS. HAWKINS in her hand and "mission accomplished" on her face. (There is a rule that no child shall run in the corridor, but such rules were not made for girls like Brooke.) This name-wearing is a nice substitute for the spoken word, and the children's use of it is a clear demonstration of their quickness and delight in reading when it serves them well. As time went by and more interesting affairs took over, the name tags properly receded, but we could well have introduced name tags for a wide range of objects with no drill necessary.*

We walked together from the cafeteria down the hall to the classroom. Hamster was waiting in his cage where I had put it in the middle of the classroom floor. Last week no one paid much attention to him. Today Greg held him briefly. Brooke was more timid and just watched, I suspect, not wanting to feel the fur. Others enjoyed feeding him lettuce and sunflower seeds which Hamster obligingly ate or stowed away in his ample cheeks. (He is often too full to eat.) The children laughed and giggled at him, and this time he stayed awake off and on during the morning. In spite of his inborn nocturnal habits this fellow was so responsive and gentle today that I shall try him again next week. While the children were playing with Hamster they often looked to Miss M., but this time I felt it was to *share* the pleasure with her rather than to ask approval for their actions. It is an important difference.

Late in the morning Patty, who had been busy with other things earlier, looked at the white hamster, ran across the room, and rummaged under dolls and blankets in a buggy. What was she doing? I certainly did not know. She had indicated that her concern had something to do with Hamster—but what? With a broad grin on her face, and arm outstretched, she returned to the group around Hamster. In her hand was a small white stuffed animal, really very much like Hamster himself. We all laughed and shared the joke. Patty had brought it from home and I believe she made a plan when she came across that small stuffed animal there. Having brought it to school she misplaced it in play, but remembered it just in time while the

* See the story of Hamster in Visit 4.

live hamster was still the focus of our attention. With no language for explanation, the exact sequence of events must remain obscure, but the essence is what counts, and this we all enjoyed. Patty cannot *say* about a white stuffed animal, "This is like Hamster!" But this has not curtailed her ability to shape her expression, to make her point, with all the attendant byproducts of learning and laughter.*

Such happy coincidences are only partly accidental. They occur more often when they are expected, valued, enjoyed, and written about. A parent or teacher who cares learns to read actions as well as words as indications that a child has matters of great import to communicate because he understands the logic behind the action. Patty here made her contribution to a good conversation, enacting a sentence, or perhaps a paragraph, with clarity, style, and humor. One appreciates the desire of any child to connect the values of home and school, but here where discussion is almost impossible our hats are off to Patty.

Even with so few children in our class the speed of action is too fast for us to see and capture many such episodes in this detail. I submit this one as a paradigm of what is to be valued here, of what I count as positive in evaluating any morning for a child—in estimating the climate of a morning itself.†

The excitement level was high later in the morning, and I feared for Hamster left unprotected, so I began to build a fence of large kindergarten blocks around him. This kind of shift of interest will tend to quiet things down, and, in catching another facet of the children's interest, leads to innovation. It did not lead to much this time though it did become quieter; and as often happens

* Here is an example of association—a story could easily have been used in the "language arts."

† A morning used by these children to give abundant clues in their actions of what was going on in their minds. Clues need not be precise to be useful for planning.

with the young, something was filed away. The fence idea
cropped up later when an inflated tire tube was used to
fence in Hamster, and even later for a visiting puppy.

Miss M. spoke to me in a joking-serious way about
Lisa during the morning: "The day I see that one involved and not asking for attention, *that* will be the day!"
I asked her to turn around and look; Lisa was blowing
bubbles with quiet and sustained involvement. We
laughed and the prognosis seemed good. It has begun to
happen to Lisa—and will, more and more.

Claire's first notes: *

> Lisa came at once to the middle of the room where the
> new plastic tub for bubbles was sitting. She mimicked to
> me that we were now going to blow bubbles, blowing
> toward me with a pretended straw. I sat on the floor and
> blew real bubbles with her for a long time. She liked hav-
> ing someone near. Also, she liked to clean up the floor
> when she spilled water, and then to neatly fold and put
> the wet paper towel in a coffee can.

Yes, Lisa still is sometimes so busy cleaning up that
she has little time left for more imaginative activities.

Most but not all of the children were unable to use
these open-ended materials except in a stereotyped or directly imitative way today. I began to judge such behavior
compulsive. Ordinarily when material responds to a
child's manipulation, evidencing its physical properties,
the child responds in turn to these phenomena, and, as I
have said, the character of this response is often of critical
importance for a teacher. If the response is merely the
next link in a chain of behavior that has already become
habitual, then there is little evidence of deep involvement or discrimination. If the response is merely imitative, one judges that attention lies elsewhere than on the

---

* Claire's notes and later those of Miss B. when quoted directly are
indented throughout the text.

material at hand, and again there is little discrimination or learning.*

Sometimes the particular thing chosen by a child is not after all his cup of tea, and he seems temporarily to lose the ability to make a search for what will be. Perhaps he has had troubles at home. In any event, something interferes with the coupling between child and material, which we know he has great capacity for. A teacher has a unique role here.† It is not the role of mother or therapist or peer, but that of one who values learner and learning professionally and wants to help that child regain and develop his capacity to probe and test, to summon his sleeping resources of imagery, control, and understanding—in short, to learn not memorize. In this process home troubles can recede because learning is sustaining in its own way. And here there is at least one tangible, sure-fire aid: if the adult in the situation is himself simultaneously and genuinely exploring the material (and not just observing how the child uses it), then a bridge may be started to the child's reinvolvement—involvement being contagious often. This is as valid a reason as any I know for having in a classroom enough materials with challenging possibilities. Is it utopian to propose that our teachers be permitted and expected to learn too? I have known teachers who first developed interests in science, at their own level, because of their perception of children's needs.

The reactions to bubble tubes is worth noting for evidence of change in the children's observation. These tubes, already filled with water and sealed, were offered last week; the children held and tilted them and watched the bubbles rise. This week we provided them a chance to make their own. There were many trips to the lavatory

* Here discrimination and learning refer to bubbles themselves: shapes, frailty, rainbow colors, movement of film, slippery feel of soap-water, ways to break bubbles or move them, catch them.

† See Anna Freud, "The Role of the Teacher," *Harvard Educational Review* 22 (1952): 229–34.

for water as the children found that it took more than one
plastic glassful to fill a long tube, and we had confirmation of our decision to include corks of *various* diameters.
There was much trial and error in the selection of corks.
Some went down the tubes; some had to be poked
through the narrower tubes, but there was much satisfaction in the final matching.

Though we think of our work as open-ended, these
tubes must not be! There is a right way and a wrong way
in the context of fitting corks as there is in solving any
equation. But *who* is to decide about the sequence? Not
always the teacher—and not, we pray, the designer of
science kits for the preschool. (Notice as we go along the
growing assurance of certain children with respect to
measuring diameters.) On this second working morning
some children were conscious of differences in size of
tubes' diameters but were not yet skilled in fitting or
matching with hand or eye.

Up to this stage in our work most suggestions of new
steps in corking and filling and uncorking had to come
from us, and the exciting long process itself was threat-
ened in this setting by normal minor accidents such as
clean water on the floor. Liquids are anathemas to public
schools!

But Greg was engrossed. After corking his tube and
thus capturing his bubble, he turned it and turned it to
watch the bubble rise. Later for a joke I tried to "catch"
the bubble, as it rose, by putting my hand around the
tube, adding a little to the still sparse repertoire of things
to invent with tubes. He appreciated the humor of this fu-
tile effort and we grinned together. It will take time for
the children to realize that not all things have to be demonstrated by the teacher, but they will begin to bring their
instincts for imaginative play to these materials, or so I
read their reactions thus far. We will still have to intervene, to invent, but less and less and not for long, except

when it adds substantively to their own exploration.*

Early in the day I had put the Attribute Blocks on a back table. When there seemed an appropriate interval I went to that table, where Patty joined me. Almost at once she sorted the blocks by color and was intrigued by the attribute of color. When I opened the package of colored nylon string loops she immediately grabbed for them.

As still often happens, the other children began to crowd around, but Patty was unable to share her new pleasure and the chance to explore. She gathered up as many blocks and loops as possible and removed them to a smaller table, away from the crowd. This seemed a sensible move and I protected her right to work there alone. She spread out the colored loops and proceeded to do a careful matching, putting each block in the loop of its own color. Janie went over to her later, took a long assessing look at the game, and joined in. Patty was aware of and grateful for Janie's care in first figuring out the rules, and accepted her assistance with satisfaction. Janie, in turn, was careful in the beginning to solicit Patty's approval for each move. They are quite a pair—no language, so much communication and inventiveness. The ways of this twosome, together and apart, were to delight us in the weeks that followed.

This morning Miss M. told a charming story about Brooke. One day recently Brooke went to a quiet corner of the room to "read." Hardly was she settled with her book when all the other children joined her. She tried to build a little wall of blocks and books but they climbed over it. Finally, with a look of resignation on her face, she put down the book and joined the play as if to say, "No chance to read today with so many curious children around."

* See Greg and Phillip at a later day with tubes and water (pp. 108–9). Also Patty's developing exploration of new ideas around these plastic tubes on pp. 71–72 and again on p. 92. Consider when and how a teacher might well bring in language—written, spoken.

On the trip home I briefed Claire on how today compared with earlier visits: many more throat sounds than I had previously heard. This seemed so whether the children were angry about turns or excitedly pleased.

We discussed the question of a teacher's intervention as it came up in this visit. In the matter of helping with tubes and corks the answer is obvious. In the question of my play with Greg, those with conventional laissez-faire principles might well frown with disapproval. I have suggested my reasons for the intervention. But I might add that I enjoy those bubbles that "fall" upward as much as any child. In sharing such enjoyment with a child there is a communication of the fact that as observers and learners we are of the same stuff. To be present but unresponsive often communicates a failure to value. To say, as we all do at times, "That's nice" or "Very good" or "Good for you" is such a meager way to evidence interest.*

This morning I tried as usual to be guided by what I believed to be last week's feedback: continuation with similar materials but with variations introduced by me if necessary. The children explored and experimented more with the water tubes and corks after seeing us do so. By the end of the morning they settled in and brought more initiative to their own choices.

Claire's observations should be added to the day's configuration:

> Funny thing about names. My name was written on a card CLAIRE and the children couldn't understand why there was no prefix, Miss or Mrs. . . . I was an adult and all the other adults had prefixes. Lisa and I sat on the floor together. I would write CLAIRE and she would leap with joy and point to me. Then I would write LISA and she would point to herself. Others joined and this went on and on.

* The dynamics of communication (here sharing pleasure over a natural phenomenon) might be separated for thought: Suppose there *is* only cursory observation by an adult. It takes a sturdy well-on-his-way four-year-old to refuse the implicit message—*nothing* worth examining here.

And—to Speak

□ ■ □ ■ □ ■ □ ■ □ ■ □ ■ □ ■ □ ■ □ ■ □ ■ □ ■ □ ■ □ ■ □ ■ □ ■ □ ■ □ ■ □ ■

VISIT 4, FEBRUARY 17

New Equipment

two flashlights with batteries in place

food color (red, yellow, blue, green) in squeeze bottles (1½ ounces mixed with water)

large, clear plastic prescription jars with lids (about 4 ounces)

When we came into the classroom this morning, our arms as usual overflowing with junk, the children were still in the reading corner working at "Who is here?" and "Who is not here?" There were sustained and loud greetings by throat sounds as the children sat and stared at us with eyes shining and smiles on every face. We made quite a sight, I am sure, with tire tube, pump, large baskets, and Hamster. I put down all but Hamster and went to the children with the cage in hand. They were delighted to have Hamster join the circle and I asked Miss M. if we could make a sign for HAMSTER IS HERE to go under the heading "Who is here?" By her hesitation, and by her previous failure to use any of the new words that have been popping up in our visits, I realized that Miss M.

does not—cannot—see any connection between her role and ours. She had made it clear that we were welcome in her classroom, but apparently in her view our work was not in the province of the "language arts" she taught the children.

To Make a Bubble-Color Tube

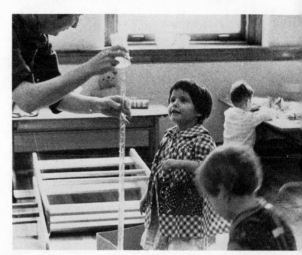

1. A squeeze bottle squeezes a little water into Brooke's long tube.

2. Then Brooke pours more water through a funnel to fill her tube almost to the top.

3. What color, Patty?

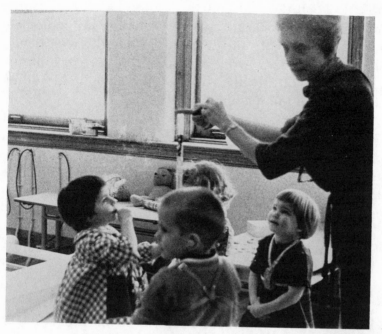

4. Down go the blue
drops slowly, slowly.

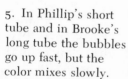

5. In Phillip's short
tube and in Brooke's
long tube the bubbles
go up fast, but the
color mixes slowly.

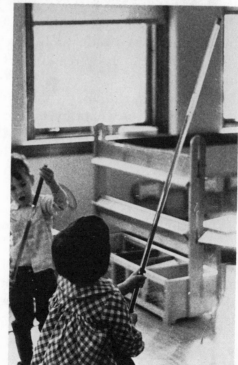

With more experience Miss M. might realize that in order to keep life and growth in a formal reading corner there must be constant association with the immediate and active world of young children. From these particular children we already had a significant directive to continue expansion at the reading board: their delight in adding new names to the reading list.

I was discouraged by Miss M.'s reluctance but thought it would be of no help to push. Perhaps I was wrong not to, but at that time I wished to maintain her pleasure in our presence and the lack of tension. These I judged more valuable than any point I might try to score by underlining that she and I were actually playing in the same ball park.

Milk and cookies again rescued us and with our names pinned on we trooped into the cafeteria where center stage was taken by the one other nursery school for deaf children at Fillmore. It happened in this way. Miss M. asked me to notice a certain Bobby at the next table: "His teacher wanted me to ask you for help with him. Some think he is brain-damaged. . . . He is becoming a real troublemaker . . . and a problem child . . . not able to sit still and profit from lip-reading." So I turned to four-year-old Bobby.

I looked at him and at the five other children at the next table, all of whom by this time were well aware of our scrutiny and were reacting to it with glances and giggles. (I had once seen this group linger wistfully in passing our open door on their way through the corridor.) Their baffled young teacher now stood a few feet away in the entrance to the cafeteria. To be rid of what was inherently a rude situation—our staring and talking about our neighbors—I moved to their table to sit with them, trying to begin communication through what was there: cookies and milk. I sat next to Bobby who was sucking his milk through a straw from the opaque carton *and* trying to watch, through the small opening, the level of milk go down; not, I thought, a stupid effort nor one which reflected anything but the boredom of an inquiring mind. I tried, with him, to see the milk go down in the carton. After a few moments, in a mischievous and testing manner Bobby started a game of hide-and-seek in that large, almost empty cafeteria. I joined in the game, to the amazement and pleasure of both groups of children. (Our six at another table just observed the play.) The facial expressions of Bobby's classmates changed during the game from testing-sly looks to the look of children unselfconsciously having fun. At the moment when I knew we'd had enough I took the children to their teacher who had been watching, much more amazed than the children. Claire observes:

> This game had its sad side too because it was obvious it was the most exciting thing that the children had done or would do for a long time. Our Miss M. said, "What if anyone comes in!"

I had about a minute to speak to Bobby's teacher and merely reported that whether or not Bobby had brain damage I couldn't say, but that all the children were terribly pent-up and in need of activity. "Pent-up?" she questioned. "But why?"

I had a chance later that morning to talk with her, and I did not know for whom to feel sorrier, the teacher or her children. She was quite defenseless about her ignorance of young children and had not the sketchiest notion of what ordinary threes and fours are like or in need of. She is not alone in this world where anyone with a Ph.D. (and a reading knowledge of B. F. Skinner or Erik Erikson) can become a designer of "new methods" for teaching the "disadvantaged"—no experience required. The young teacher defended the lip-reading-at-length exercises as the thing to be doing with these deaf children; she knew no other. To be of any help in this offhand way was impossible, and I felt that I was being just another if less ugly threat to this already frightened young teacher by bringing up a dimension she had not consciously known: that any children—deaf, blind, or "normal"—must be studied and their classrooms designed around their needs and levels of development.

(In the weeks that followed, this group of children had more and more troubles: tantrums and crying, and misery on the face of their teacher. I tried not to listen or notice as I walked by that room, but there is a poignant end to this long aside which must be told. One Thursday, as Bobby's class loitered by our open door, we invited them in and they had turns with some of our stuff. I felt like an ogre not letting them stay and "play in our garden," but in this public school it was not my place to rule on such affairs. We always felt like trespassers at Fillmore until we got inside Miss M.'s room. After this particular morning Bobby's teacher stopped me in the corridor. "Mrs. Hawkins, I wish you would come and work with my children once a week." Such an S.O.S. should be answered somehow in our vast, rich school system. But I was there for one class, adjunct of one special project, and already on notice—the details I omit—that my position carried with it no generalized welcome to the school.)

We brought flashlights today. Too often these are just turned on and off and never opened. To introduce them, then , I turned one flashlight on and off, unscrewed the end, took out the batteries and spring, put them back, and turned it on again. I arranged this "daring" demonstration just before it was time for milk. Phillip's curiosity must have held through milk time, because once back in the classroom he and Greg headed for the flashlights.

Phillip immediately opened the end, removed the batteries, replaced them, and slid the button to ON. No uncertainty here about which end of the batteries was "up."

Greg took the other flashlight and proceeded to do the same, but not without a will-we-be-permitted-to-do-it? look. Both boys were more interested in the repetition of taking apart and putting together than in turning on the light, but they *always* got the batteries in the right way.

The flashlights were theirs to open and explore and learn from. I regret that I did not provide them with wires, small bulbs, buzzers (which can be felt as well as heard), small motors, and extra batteries. At that time I had not explored enough myself with these materials. Since then I have had the chance to work with African children who taught me how useful the whole array of batteries and bulbs can be with older children, and at a younger level, Head Start fours have amazed me and delighted themselves with the possibilities of these materials. (Constant concern, of course, for removing dead batteries.)

I ask myself how I could have missed seeing the potential here at Fillmore. Those battery-run hearing aids could have been an intricate part of such a tangent, one to be seen in another light and learned about. So—teachers must learn too, and perhaps someone will see from my experience how not to do things and how to have some fun with deaf children and buzzers, bulbs, and batteries. As gold mines sometimes are, this one is rich if not structured and reduced to "How to Light a Bulb."

Greg finally went to pump air into a tire. This might have been a good time to work alone with Phillip, to find out more about him, but he had so far shown no need and I hesitated to interfere when a small boy on his own was directing his mind so well with new materials.

Claire catches a fuss:

A little trouble developed over the tire tube with Brooke, Janie, and Greg, who refused to give up the tube. Mrs. Hawkins averted a fight between Brooke and Greg by telling Greg at least to give a turn to Janie, who was less demanding than Brooke, or else he would have to put the tube and pump away. All this was easily and immediately communicated by words, objects, and facial expression. Greg agreed, gave Janie a turn, and then even Brooke. * We definitely need more than one tube next time. Lisa started to play with the Creature Set from the Attribute Blocks all by herself. So far I have seen her play only when people were near and watching.

It is clear that in introducing a totally new activity a decision is made by the teacher about how much and what kind of structure will accompany it. Let me use as an example my thinking about introducing food color for these children. The cluster of materials here, while including water as something known and recently enjoyed, is still inherently new to most children and esthetically vivid. The road to chaos can be short. It has been my experience that there is more employment and exploration if the introduction of food color is "structured." On this particular morning, when I decided to turn to the back table where the food color and related materials were waiting, I made another judgement. A time for quieter activity with teacher involved was needed. Had the early part of the morning followed another kind of pattern, I might have canceled these plans. On a Monday morning, for example, after a cold and confining weekend, I have found children so deeply in need of self-direction in familiar paths, with adults far in the background, that I have put away "structured" plans. Guidance at such times courts trouble, competes with needs of higher priority, and solidifies a reaction of wandering attention.

Having decided to introduce color drops and water in a careful fashion, I knew that until the curtain went up

* Greg could thus share yet save face, and showed us by his generous later behavior that he was ready to go even further.

there was the possibility that the children's response might prove me wrong. I have seen too many children delighted and learning with these food colors to hazard pushing it through if such responses were not present this time, and I was prepared to retreat if necessary.

The table was covered with newspaper, and each child had two five-inch-tall plastic jars ready to be filled with clear water. I was custodian of the four plastic squeeze bottles, each containing a different color, and initially helped each child squeeze a drop or three or four into his own water. Finally, when the children were obviously involved with the phenomena, I realized on the spot that this was a great opportunity to try some language, so I encouraged some to ask for a particular color. Patty, Lisa, and Phillip tried to ask half-successfully (half in that they tried at all). Brooke ignored this challenge, but watch her with color drops in Visit 6. Since language was inherent in the situation so long as I kept the colors in hand, and laughter in the throats, efforts to name the colors continued. I kept those colors in hand. A time would come for another kind of exploration of these materials.

Claire notes:

More verbalization today, especially when the children were sitting around the table to work with colors in their plastic jars. In addition to their "Oh"s and "Ah"s at seeing the colors in the water, I heard Janie ask for "blue" quite distinctly and carefully, and Greg asked for "yellow."

During this sequence I was reassured by the children's ease in waiting and taking turns that the change from freewheeling to quiet plan was appropriate. It felt right to everyone. The intrinsic richness of color swirls mixing and changes of color density held magic for us all.

After we had left the table, when the others were using long bubble tubes, Patty transformed her small jar.

Claire watches:

> There just weren't enough long bubble tubes to go around,
> so Patty used her plastic jar with its lid for a short bubble
> tube and didn't complain about not getting a long one to
> work with. She had put pale green water in her jar, which
> showed the bubble beautifully, and she was content to tilt
> the short jar-tube from side to side and watch her bubble
> go up and down.

I want to speak about Lisa for a moment. Her behavior
during the morning regressed to her former attention-
seeking and Miss M. reported that at the end of the previous Thursday Lisa had been terribly fatigued and
frayed. One need not assume that this was caused by our
presence, but I prefer not to sidestep in that way.

During last week's visit, in spite of the addition of
another adult to Lisa's sphere of school (perhaps because
of it), she was able at times to forget adults and lose herself in an activity. But those brief moments were more indicative of the future than of the present for her. She is
not yet able to use her energy to explore the new dimension of free choice because most of that energy is still
needed to bid for her old sustainers—praise, direction,
personal notice. Not having developed enough genuine
interest in the materials themselves, disassociated from
the persons who bring them, her energy is constantly
drained by our very presence and her attempts to change.
This kind of fatigue, genuine though it is, may be a positive signal of growth. Frederick Allen first alerted me to
this possibility. He states: "An increase of inner struggle
before a leave-taking or breakthrough is not uncommon." * I have found this so in similar classroom situa-

* For further discussions of these matters, see *Psychotherapy with
Children*, pp. 269–73. This one book out of many in the field has
proved itself again and again in meeting with positive analysis the
kinds of problems a teacher encounters in children each day.

tions over many years. We shall see how it goes with Lisa.

Phillip's behavior today was in particular contrast to Lisa's. He was a dreamer but not unhappy or bored. He set his own slow pace at tasks which interested him. He was fond of Hamster and really the most affectionate and gentle of all the children, as though he could already feel *for* another creature in a more mature manner than the others could.

I had a final view of Brooke wandering down the hall in her most withdrawn way. Her involvement today was shallow and disturbing. She is the one who needs my most careful thinking.

Claire's indignation met me as I got into the car. She had been waiting there for a few minutes watching the playground.

> I noticed on the playground today what seemed an inordinate amount of fighting between older kids. Kids were pushing children who had hearing aids in their ears. In general the yard didn't seem a bit pleasant.

On the drive home we tried to sort out some of the implications. Claire's immediate ire was against the children who were pushing the deaf. But I had only to remind her of the behavior of Bobby's class as an example of what results in all children from frustration and boredom in classrooms. "Of course," she realized, "the hearing kids must be pent-up and bored too. Our Miss M. is probably the best teacher in the school." A playground is such a true projection of inner, personal matters.

Our Classroom

No, I don't want any more kindergarten materials. I used my little stock of beads, cards, and straws at first because I didn't know what else to do. . . . I am beginning to suspect all elaborate and special systems of education. They seem to me to be built up on the supposition that every child is a kind of idiot who must be taught to think. . . . Let him go and come freely, let him touch real things and combine his impressions for himself.

—Ann Sullivan
from a letter to Perkins Institute in
Helen Keller, *Story of My Life*

Enough Junk

▫ ◼ ▫ ◼ ▫ ◼ ▫ ◼ ▫ ◼ ▫ ◼ ▫ ◼ ▫ ◼ ▫ ◼ ▫ ◼ ▫ ◼ ▫ ◼ ▫ ◼ ▫ ◼ ▫ ◼ ▫ ◼

VISIT 5, FEBRUARY 25 (Greg absent)

New Equipment

plastic wading pool (3 foot diameter) and toys: syringes, coffee pots, plastic Rx jars

tire tubes, many this morning including a couple of bicycle tubes

gels—six colors (red, orange, blue, yellow, green, purple) made of colored plastic transparent gel material used for theater lighting. Each gel was 3 inches x 5 inches with rounded corners and edged with masking tape. On the taped edge of each gel we wrote the name of its color.*

The children were already drinking their milk when we walked by the cafeteria today. We tiptoed down that silent hall with arms full, and the eagle eyes of our six missed us.

* See Appendix 2 for more recent information about gels.

Claire went back to the cafeteria while I stayed in the classroom to set up the equipment. In this setting it was a luxury to do so—but one I usually count indispensable. At the end of one session I am not ready to think of the next, being too concerned with reliving what has just happened. The luxury-necessity of being in my own classroom alone just before the children come in gives me a time when the worth of five consecutive minutes is incalculable. Clues and implications from the previous day's work are everywhere and the silence-with-time permits me to see and weave those suggestive clues into the next scene.

The inflatable wading pool was new today, planned as a holding place for overflow water from the tubes. No one took *that* plan seriously. Phillip, who usually goes to the heart of a matter, marched to the pool, sat himself down as close as possible without getting in, and looked at the cans of water I had placed in it. With speed and little ceremony he dumped all of the water into the pool. Babies are christened with a gentle sprinkling. Phillip, I suspect, will christen hulls, which takes gusto.

I look at Claire's photograph of Phillip and muse about him. He exemplifies those children who become adults with much knowledge of and great joy in the natural phenomena of our world—stars or otters, electricity as it is explored by a kite on the end of a string, or the pattern of many reflections of a light from wavelets on water. Somewhere in childhood such people learn how to observe and to try their hands long enough at one thing to establish a beginning—even as Phillip does here. Watch him.

After the scramble for tire tubes last time, we brought for today every old patched tire tube our local gas station could find and mend. The children used them at intervals throughout the morning in foreseen and unforeseen ways. They were pumped up and deflated (with much ado over

valve stems and the feel of air as it was released); the tires
were again pumped up, sat in, rolled, rolled on, patted,
and then much of this all over again. What I call a nesting
syndrome was tripped when several children just sat
snugly inside a tire tube with their four-year-old backs
nicely propped and legs akimbo. For minutes on end they
sat thus inside the tube enjoying this protected place from
which they looked out at the world through the colored
gels—or so their behavior told us.

Claire observed:

> When we came back to the room Brooke went at once to
> the tire pump and pumped up one of the large tubes.
> When she finally noticed everyone else at the new water
> pool she too went to the pool. There Lisa had already
> filled and corked a long bubble tube and was turning it
> from side to side watching the bubble go up. Brooke
> joined Lisa and made her own tube, corking and filling it
> with water. After it was corked she spent a long time
> watching her own bubble. The children often still look to
> the teacher for cues or permission when they want to
> change from one activity to another. At the water pool, for
> example, they seek approval to use a syringe instead of
> pouring.

Everyone tried his hand at the water pool this morning, but Phillip and Janie were the two who stayed and
whose actions we can report. We missed the details of
Phillip's initial water play after the christening, and that
makes me sad. But we caught some of Janie's, which com-
pensates. Phillip, unaware of anyone's scrutiny, would fill
his large plastic syringe with water by pulling out the
plunger while the tip was submerged, and then shoot the
water to the opposite side of the pool. He was expert at
controlling the force and speed on his plunger as he
aimed the small stream.

Janie kept watching Phillip's actions. Quite obviously

she wanted to do the same thing with her syringe, but she was unable to fill it with water, the first step in this desirable sequence. (Her trouble here is not unique to four-year-olds. We have watched adults at the Mountain View Center, like Janie unused to syringes, get hung up on the identical set of reverse motions. They pull out the plunger in the air, put the tip of the syringe-tube into water, then push the plunger down. Nice bubbles rise to the surface, but the syringe does not fill with water.)

After some interest in the unplanned bubbles, Janie turned again to watch how Phillip got water into that stubborn syringe. Then, say Claire's notes, "She *thought* about it." With syringe out of the pool she pushed down the plunger, then put the tip in the pool and slowly pulled up the water into the transparent syringe. The final part of the sequence, shooting water across the pond, proceeded, but Janie's success in using eyes, hands, and mind to fill the syringe was for her, I submit, an achievement of equal merit. To write about it is in some degree to share her pleasure.

It may be useful to spell out the less tangible implications of this episode. One catches too few. Both children, one notes, are nibbling at some very nice pieces of the real world: a liquid state of matter, volume, space, the reality of air, force, time. We can say that in some sense children do this all the time. But whether our schools appreciate and encourage this kind of engagement by providing time and equipment for children *and* their teachers is a question. We have watched teachers in our laboratory, with no children present, letting themselves explore with color, water, mirrors, mobiles, balances, and pendulums. They are amazed and delighted at the pleasure which accompanies their learning. Others, of course, stand by writing notes in their notebooks, looking for lesson plans or magic formulas, unable to touch and try. Though they may have college degrees they are deprived.

It is not easy for teachers to provide for a kind of learning they do not know and appreciate themselves from experience. I digress here to make a plea not only for children, who suffer when a teacher does, but for the many teachers I meet who are unhappy, bored, and lost.

There are still more aspects of this episode with Janie to be noted. Setting of goals is one. To shoot water across the pool might be called a self-set goal for Janie, but it was not, as the task developed, one that interfered with savoring and exploring along the way. Consider the absence of frustration in her failures. Does this have to do with the fact that a child not yet taught otherwise by school keeps his goal in mind as he loiters along the way—testing, learning, seeking to understand? And suppose he changes his goal—is this the "sin" we are programming out? Add extrinsic rewards to preconceived "behavioral objectives" replacing Janie's kind of self-set enterprise, where failure and success on her own terms lead toward understanding a small facet of the world's mystery; make just that change and watch to see what in fact has been subtracted from the primary need to understand and create. Children learn something in operant conditioning experiments—it is their very nature to learn—but how narrow is the learning, how wasteful and minor in the scope of what man must learn to survive as joyous man!

Consider sequence and order here for Janie. Such terms, if not called concepts, are much in the minds of those who work at programmed learning for our young. In all of the search to find *the one* proper order I miss any awareness of the existing levels for such important and really basic concepts. There is an obvious and thin layer of sequence which has to do with the minutiae of life such as catching a bus (or reading its number). If one arrives at the proper corner one minute after the bus has left, one misses it. This can be annoying, but the remedy is obvi-

ous and though we sometimes miss a bus (or misplace an
overcoat along with Mr. Thurber), we do not therefore
and necessarily miss the more important conveyances or
absolutely misplace the necessities of our lives. Preoccupation with minutiae, substitution of rote memorization
for learning, parroting back answers, smiling when the
teacher says "smile"—this kind of sequential nonsense
will undermine the learning capacity of our *most vulnerable* young. It will certainly greatly decrease the chances
that they will be able to catch the most important
"buses," whose schedules are partly written by each new
generation as it comes in contact with the real world.

Order or sequence in Janie's learning exists in this incident but only in retrospect can one define it. Early on it
must have been clear to her that *before* she could squirt
water out of her syringe there must be water in it. This
was not an insignificant sense of fundamental order for
her to build on. From there how did she proceed? Knowing she must *do* something, she tried to get the water in
by pulling out the plunger before immersing the syringe.
Failure resulted, though the bubbles compensated a little.
She must have been satisfied at this point that the successful Phillip possessed some particular piece of knowledge which eluded her. After watching Phillip, she tried
again—and failed. More observation, some thought about
it, and she was *in.* There is much more here than dreamed
of in a programmed lesson "How to Work a Hand Pump."

And back to Phillip who followed the beat of his own
drum and stayed at the wading pool a very long time after
Janie left, quietly engrossed with the water and syringe,
trying, testing, spilling, squirting. My first day's picture of
him returns when I reread these notes: that bored, restless but obedient little boy on a chair in the reading corner, his only defense in the situation being to daydream
or halfheartedly examine the nearby wall.

Claire adds:

I noticed Phillip take a chair and go to play with the new
large magnetic letters (provided by Miss M.) which were
sticking to a magnetic board hung in the reading corner.
He stayed there taking the letters off, sticking them on,
and moving them around all by himself until Patty came
and played beside him for a good fifteen minutes. Both
children were much more interested in the magnetism
than in the symbolism of the letters. Phillip found the
magnifier-with-light and examined the large letters carefully.

I wonder whether Phillip hoped to find out why those
letters stuck, or whether he noticed the magnifier and
used it in a random way with no thoughts about what
made the letters stick. Knowing a little about how Phillip
puts things to work for his understanding of the world, I
would like to believe the former.

The introduction of gels went something like this. I sat
on the floor holding six gels of different colors in my
hand, and beckoned the children to join me. Greg was absent, so there were five children. I had given one gel to
each when Lisa, who seldom misses this sort of number
difference, took the extra gel from my hand and superimposed it on hers. Her reaction, after looking through the
two, was pure delight.

We had made the six gels for general use, not thinking
particularly of providing one gel for each child, but I realized quickly from the children's immediate and covetous
reaction that the gels would not become general equipment to be shared. Children have a way of communicating a *fait accompli* about such matters leaving no
doubt as to the course they dictate.

Claire watched Lisa:

I saw Lisa take a gel to the long mirror and look at herself
through it. She laughed at herself with gel over eyes and
then removed it and laughed at herself again. Brooke
looked through hers, then carried it to the reading corner,

where she found her name in the envelope and slipped her gel in beside it.

Sometime later in the morning Brooke and I had a complicated wordless "conversation" about the gels. She came to me and tried to explain something with gestures. Preoccupied, I did not follow her logic or realize what she was pointing to in my pocket. I had in fact forgotten that I had put the extra gel there to save for Greg. Brooke gestured and looked me in the eye as if to say, "This is important; please listen." I tried but didn't understand, so she led me to the reading corner. Turning to the board she found what she was seeking and ran her finger under it: GREG IS NOT HERE. Then she turned to me, pointed to the gel in my pocket, and I finally understood. Yes, I nodded, this gel is for Greg who is not here, and I will save it for him. Brooke smiled broadly and walked away with a lilt in her step. Sometimes, I imagined her saying to herself, it *is* possible to communicate with that usually nonunderstanding world.

Claire writes:

> Lisa was magnificent with a tire tube. She pumped it up all by herself, which took a long time. She was very pleased with her effort. Brooke demanded a turn with the pump and Mrs. H. interfered.

Brooke in her most persuasive manner tried to get Lisa to give her the pump, but when Lisa, so often unengaged, is this much involved I feel she should be protected. At the end of the morning Lisa had more trouble and cried over the blocks. Miss M. held her and comforted her in her lap, and Brooke who had cornered some gels came over to Lisa and offered her one! (Nice commentary on Miss M.'s personal relationship with these children.)

We stayed to meet some of the mothers this morning, and they too were inordinately interested in the gels.

NOTES ON THIS MORNING'S VISIT

As in other kinds of regular sessions (therapy, music lessons) which are designed for continuity and have some sense of building, the rhythm of what we are doing here is beginning to be felt and variations designed. Let me assess some things about Brooke as an example, thinking, in particular, about her concern for Greg's gel.

First, she is using that remarkable mind to make order of our presence. She now knows certain important things about us and something of what this means in her school world. That we bring materials worth her time and her anticipation has become obvious before now by her participation. But suddenly in this session, she finds it worthwhile to try to communicate with me about important but difficult ideas. This is a new and heady dimension in our brief association; it indicates the thinking this small girl so often has locked up inside. A two-way relationship is developing which goes beyond the one-way flow in which I supply her with equipment and things to do.

Specifically, I speculate that Brooke thought we had brought a gel for each child and needed to indicate her appreciation of our planning for everyone including the absent Greg. This, though partly subconscious, is intrinsically rich. There is so much more in this brief episode: beginning understanding of the logical roots of cardinal numbers, of one-to-one correspondence, of the use of written language to point out a subtlety about the morning which Brooke could not otherwise communicate. In addition, this is a kind of positive bridge-building between the other four days' learning and the one morning we are here, and Brooke is doing it herself.

Only in retrospect do I realize that just here I should have been alerted to how very much Brooke needed a one-to-one relationship with an adult—so that she could "talk." It is the depth of her need I missed, being too enamored with her potential. Perhaps under the circumstances I could not have supplied her need, but I want to note it here with humility because at another time and place I might miss an opportunity to understand when it *could* make a difference, where circumstances *would* permit.

About color and gels: In preschools the common evaluation of a child's knowledge of color is based on whether he can name and identify "his colors." This is one of those small but revealing commentaries which shout out to some of us about the narrowness of evaluators and of curriculums in which such learning is considered as either difficult or central to a child's familiarity with the multifaceted world of color.

All the young in my experience have been deeply appreciative of color in bubbles, crayons, paints, food, water (deep, shallow, muddy), flowers, leaves, birds, and blocks—but they are especially and most appropriately appreciative of what we call properties or attributes when they are working with *all* of these pieces of their world.

For the deaf in this particular situation, with no words to help, we had to be more inventive so that color itself would be abstracted and appreciated. This was an excellent experience for me, and though one never does navigate twice in the same way, I learned much to add to my own repertoire for color within the restrictive setting of a neat city classroom.

The gels themselves grew out of a large box of photographic gel material in 24 inch x 36 inch sheets in our lab. The children's need and search for wider activity within the world of sight tripped our own abilities to search, and so the gels we used here were discovered.*

* See Appendix 2 for new source.

As I have noted, the gels were used almost greedily this morning. There was some trading and sharing but the children kept track of their individual gels and retrieved them quickly. Once I saw how the children made these their own I knew we must make a set of six for each child. (See Visit 9 for how it went on the morning we brought the sets in envelopes.)

It is useful to speculate about why and how these were used, were invested. One keeps a keen interest in minor matters of presentation, in timing, in being aware of the setting into which one introduces a particular bit of material. Often one cannot separate out which element makes a difference in a child's reaction. This does not indicate that the totality of timing, setting, plus material cannot be usefully evaluated. When I lose awareness of these matters I find I cannot stimulate enough variation in children's own use of materials. For example: Here I wanted to protect the delicate acetate by making a rather careful presentation so that a child could exploit it well before it tore. Such care on my part invests material with some added feature that a child may initially notice. Did this kind of valuing on my part affect the children's reactions? Were the uses they made of the gels narrowed or widened by my preparation? Is there a human dimension added when a teacher values something in a special way? What kinds of materials should *not* be hedged in this way?

These are the kinds of questions I need to ask myself and to seek answers for in the children's actual responses—never mind whether I am satisfied with any one answer or whether I am certain how to anchor a particular response. If I don't vary procedure and pose such questions I remain truly at sea. After enough evidence is in from a varied stage setting there begins to appear a trend which suggests yet new directions.

A Quiet Morning
to Remember

□■■□■□□□■□■□■□■□■□■□■□■□■□■□■□■□■□■□■■□■

New Equipment

plastic eyedroppers to be used with food colors

Today was to me a completely different sort of day. There
was much more self-sustained interest, less running
around from one thing to another, and longer interest
spans for all the children. As we walked by the cafeteria
with all the equipment in our arms, there were shrieks of
joy from the children who were having their milk. Mrs. H.
stayed in the classroom to set things up while I joined
Miss M. and the children. Lisa remembered that I had
burned my arm with an iron the week before and immediately started tugging at my long sleeve to let her see the
burn. She went through the whole pantomime with much
sympathy.

Claire's observations are a good beginning for today's
notes. They catch the tone of the morning—new to Claire
(this school being her first experience with children) and
welcome to me, an old hand, as a slower tempo emerged.
For this particular morning I had planned to continue and
consolidate what was started last week and, where I felt I
had clues from the children's earlier response to new

ideas with food color, to explore that material further.

For water itself and for making and unmaking bubble tubes we brought the water pool with funnels, jars, etc. There were corks and some of the long plastic tubes. On a newspaper-covered back table were jars, water supply, food color, and the new eyedroppers. I put Attribute Blocks out on another table to provide an alternative activity which would carry itself if need be or would supply material for an adult's working with one child.

It is useful to assess materials from such points of view as an aid to flexibility in their use and in deploying staff with young children. Many tire tubes and the pump were put in another corner. These could also be managed alone or become a good thing around which a child might explore with a teacher. Against the background of concentrated and exploratory work which pervaded the morning, I choose two episodes to give further definition to a kind of developing pattern and to underline that observation is required *along the way*—that for a teacher evaluation should be built in as a guide, not superimposed by evaluators.*

The first setting was this: Greg and Phillip were quickly lost at the plastic pool in a water-world of their own, working with tubes, syringes, jars, and funnels. Greg had been absent last time and I was lucky enough to see his initial reaction to the pool when he walked in alone from the cafeteria. He stopped just inside the door, stared at the pool, pointed at it, turned toward me with what I think was a conspiratorial smile—of appreciation for my audacity in bringing such a thing to the classroom? . . . or as a confirmation of his anticipation of a surprise? I cannot

---

* One can make use of outside evaluators if they are not also the designers of the program they are testing. Let tests be designed to test narrow items—as they are only able to do for the young—but let testers not expect children and teachers to *live* narrowly.

pinpoint the meaningful look he gave me, but I valued it as approval of the pool.

With such a warm and appreciative communication—eye to eye, smile to smile—I felt safe in believing that Greg indeed was beginning to build a new and secure path into the world of school. Miss M. confirmed this later. It is nice to watch Greg carefully from here on, although it was not until Visit 10 that we had no more doubt about his embracing a wider world.

One of my intentions this morning was to remain at the back table to dispense color and encourage language. I started with the four girls who had chosen this activity. Keeping the small bottles of food color in my hand at first, I encouraged each child to ask for the color she wanted by its name. Janie laughed and was able, with repeated help, to ask for blue, then green. Patty tried happily, with less success, but unceasing effort, and Lisa, halfheartedly with little awareness and little success, moved her lips (not unlike her earlier motions-minus-logic with the light-magnifier).

I purposely didn't ask Brooke what color she wanted because this kind of participation was not, it will be remembered, her forte. Suddenly, however, she was pulling at my dress to get attention. I looked at her carefully, knowing she does not try to communicate unless it is important. She pointed first to her lips, then to mine, then to a bottle of food coloring. With excitement I put the question: "What color, Brooke?" Watching my lips carefully she answered by moving hers. This had little relation to the correct lip movement and there was no sound but it was an approximation of the finest baby talk I have ever observed an infant use for trying words that sound right. It felt right to Brooke and to me. Bravo to her!

Miss M. later told us that to her knowledge Brooke had never before done this. Children like Brooke must choose the moment.

Claire comments:

An amazing communication went on between Lisa and
Janie. Lisa mouthed something as Janie was looking at
her. Then Janie, seeming to understand, gave her some
green coloring and her own plastic jars. This happened
while Mrs. H. was asking the children what colors they
wanted.

It is nice to have these deaf children remind us so
graphically that conversation is contagious—that they are
ready to work at language as long as it belongs and adds
to their more immediate if not more vital concerns.

The second selected incident is brief. Late in the
morning the children were dropping color into the long,
water-filled tubes, and when there were many such tubes
of various colors, well corked by careful four-year-old
fingers, I borrowed Janie's tube of bright geen water and
carried it to where a stream of sunlight showed through it.
Claire describes what happened:

Janie ran after Mrs. H. and hugged the tube. Brooke joined
them, pointed to her own mouth, and wanted to say a
color; Patty took the cork out of her tube and dumped its
colored water into the pool, laughing as its color spread in
the clear water; Janie tilted her green tube and *said*, "Big
bubble."

Claire's description of clean-up time further character-
izes the morning. To keep the unrushed pace I started the
clean-up process early enough to encourage a leisurely
unwinding from the calm richness of the day's actitivites
and to allow us to continue harvesting byproducts of language and insights—the children's and ours.

It was great fun when the children started to empty colored water from their tubes into the water pool. Today
they seemed to have noticed consciously that different

corks fit different tubes—some stuck, some got lost down inside, some fit just right. Emptying water and carrying it from pool to lavatory became an activity in itself. They were helping us to clean up and looked and acted so self-important!

Claire's notes have become more useful to me over the weeks. The taste of promise was in the air for us all. Claire said it, our children acted it, and I was content.

From Bubbles Through Chaos to Invention

□■□■□■□■□■□■□■□■□■□■□■□■□■□■□■□■□■□■□■

VISIT 7, MARCH 10 (Claire absent)

New Equipment

large aluminum salt shakers filled with various noise makers: beans, seeds, rocks, etc. (Matching clear plastic containers with identical contents were also brought today but not used.)

Circumstances changed our pattern today. Claire was ill, and I had the help, for carrying things, of a young graduate student in sociology.* When one varies intentionally or inadvertently what has become routine, there is a nice opportunity to learn something new about the children themselves as they respond to the change. It was nice for all of us to have a young man around, if only briefly. Schools are so segregated.

When my friend Reyes and I came into the building with the usual paraphernalia in our arms the children were at the far end of the hall coming toward us to the cafeteria. The now familiar, loud, happy greetings of "Oh"s and "Ah"s reverberated down the long hall, but when the children came close there were questioning looks on all

* Reyes Ramos came to observe—if only briefly.

faces: "Who is that?" "What is happening?" "Where is Claire?" I went to set up in the classroom with the help of Reyes while the children had their milk, but they were upon us very soon. For the first few minutes the children stayed near me and watched our visitor. Their behavior was such a flashback to their early ways that I realized what a close friendship we have built by now.

Though bubbles were fragile and brief phenomena, they led into a vividly rich and lasting experience this morning. The children and I sat around a table for a quiet time and just blew bubbles. This is satisfying enough when one exploits the variety: big ones, tiny ones—many, few, two, three, four, and more . . . all of these with rainbow colors to be glimpsed and shapes to be popped and reblown. Communication became a natural need between friends sharing the enchantment of the delicate soap films, and with the blackboard beside us I again moved to use it as part of our attempt to "speak" to each other about what we were blowing-making-seeing. (See page 141 for a picture of earlier such use.)

Here a child's sense for form allows him to interpret even an amateur's drawings. It may be that the deaf rely upon and hence sharpen this useful interpretative ability. I drew a small hand on the board with small circles all over it and wrote underneath, "Patty made many bubbles on her hand." Then we all looked from Patty's real hand covered with bubbles to the replica on the board with understanding and much amusement.

Phillip was particularly charmed. He blew bubbles on his own hand, came to me at the board, and soon his hand, too, was etched in chalk with "Phillip made big bubbles on his hand" written underneath.

This kind of nonsense-with-sense had to be further shared, and so I drew many hands and many bubbles all over the old dusty blackboard. Somewhere in the process

of transforming real bubbles to slate and chalk it was realized that one could trace a hand on the board and then
draw circles and circles and more circles all over one's
own traced hand. This led to further invention. Large
paper went down on the floor so that feet could be traced
and individual legends written nearby: "Lisa's foot . . .
Janie's foot . . ."

Suddenly in all this mirth I came sharply up against
that steel wall of deafness. I wanted so to tell the children, *just then,* the old story about Abraham Lincoln
holding a child upside-down so that muddy footprints
could be made on the ceiling as a mystery-joke for his absent mother. Because the children were deaf I could not
tell it. Not being in my own classroom I couldn't run to
the library corner and get the d'Aulaire *Abraham Lincoln*
to show the children. Later I remembered Ezra Keats's
The Snowy Day which also would have added still more
to this lovely morning with its description of prints of feet
and sticks in snow.

It is inevitable that chances are lost because sharp
turns and new tangents are so frequent among the young.
But here the loss was compounded by deafness, by the
long week between visits, and by our not being able to
supply the room with background materials and a good
library, which meet such emergencies. The best authors
of books for young children understand the close coupling
of action with language for the under-fives and rely properly on all the senses as media of communication in the
creation of classics.

We went on to other matters and turned for the first
time to the aluminum shakers containing various small
objects: rice in one, peas, sand, or rocks in others. (See
Appendix 2 for further description.) The sound and feel
which came through that thin bottom when each can was
shaken separately was distinctly indicative of the shape

Shakers with—

dry peas and brown beans
sunflower seeds and rice
lima beans and tapioca
big rocks and sand.

Plastic shakers to see
through.
Aluminum shakers
to feel through.

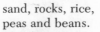

sand, rocks, rice,
peas and beans.

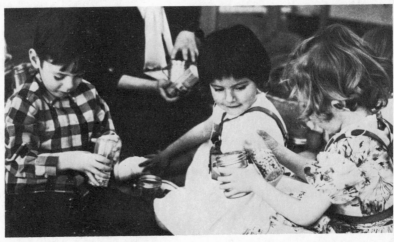

and size of what was inside, as we had found to our surprise when trying them in our lab. I was curious about their feel to a deaf child.

Interest was mild as the children first held or shook a shaker, and I judged by faces that they were mystified without being involved—as they must be by many "closed boxes" in their lives. Perhaps I should have introduced simultaneously the clear plastic containers filled with identical materials, but I wanted to make use of feel, not sight, this time around. (The pictures showing both opaque and clear shakers at the beginning of this chapter were taken during Visit 9.)

One can intervene at such a juncture when interest is not high or one can fold up plans and try again later. Being conscious of the brief time we always had with these children and still curious myself, I intervened. I selected from the shakers the two with most contrast: one with fine sand and one with rocks. Now when a child shook these two he responded with an expression of surprised pleasure at the second—no matter which came first. So far so good. The logical next step (to the children) was taken by all. No suggestions were needed. The tops of all the shakers were unscrewed in rapid succession and the floor was soon covered with peas, beans, seeds, lead shot, rocks, and sand. Watch Patty make great sense out of this chaos.

Until now she had not seemed even slightly interested in the shakers and instead had been intently busy making and exploring a long bubble tube. She had used green to color the water, just enough to accentuate the bubble, not enough to make the water opaque. She tipped and turned and watched that long, clean bubble, beautifully rounded on top, rise and rise again. With tube in one hand Patty came over to the assortment of small things from the shakers quickly spreading on the floor.

While I wondered where we went from there, she picked up with incredible dexterity some things from the mess, walked to a nearby table, and put down her chosen assortment. With obvious purpose not yet understood by any of us on the floor (but holding our attention), she uncorked the green tube. In went one dried pea, and momentarily I thought: Oh no, now we will really be in the soup with water and beans and peas on the floor. But I should have trusted Patty. She corked the tube, turned it, and watched the pea fall gently through the bubble and settle on the bottom while the bubble rose.

While most of us watched from the floor, Patty continued her experiment. In succession she dropped in, and watched fall, lead shot, a small rock, and a kernel of corn—uncorking and corking for each new inclusion. Then she picked from her gatherings a sunflower seed. To her delight and to ours the seed did not sink but was caught by the bubble and rose on top of it like a hat!

Patty had not paid us any attention until this surprise, but then she turned to me to be sure I could see the phenomenon. I read the expression on her face as: "I didn't expect *that*, did you?" Or, "How can *that* happen?" Whatever the exact formulation in her mind, we all shared the excitement and hence many bubble tubes with small "things" were made and tested. This gave us enough time to retrieve the extra small things on the floor before they could cause trouble, and I blessed another of those happy accidents.

In many of our children inventiveness is still intact when they come to school—Patty's perceptiveness underlines this here. Superimpose what programming (to reinforce the correct answer or define proper use of materials) will eliminate in such an episode: no doubt the messy floor, but certainly Patty's "misuse" of the seeds. A suggestion would be made or a light flashed: "Wrong path; the small things belong to the shakers." My own first reaction to the spill was dull and standard: Clean it up! To observe the use or misuse of our supplies and equipment during these mornings and to raise questions about the quality of the chilren's behavior exemplifies what evaluation of the young is all about. When children independently invent, recombine, and uncover new wonders (floating, sinking), we see that we are on exciting paths with them.

Late in the morning the gentle Phillip came to me with his smile just showing and offered his arm for help in rolling up his sleeves. Last week he must have enjoyed this preparation which accompanies water play because his small, self-initiated action was so obviously an expressive gesture from him to me. Then Greg sought my help, though his sleeves were really up far enough. He too, I thought, wanted to enter our sphere of communication, to be friendly. These silent children invent so well and show gratitude in the only meaningful way—by savoring all aspects of what is provided, by choosing ways to emphasize and to extend a sweet moment. After such a morning, of course, no one wishes to break the spell by leaving—not teacher, certainly.

Janie's mother came in to speak with me after class; we had just met for the first time. "Janie can't *tell* what happens when you are here," she said, "but we know from her face that you have been." She then told me that the previous Saturday Janie watched her father drinking soda pop, got very excited, pointed at the bottle and said, "Bubble . . . bubble." "So," her mother continued, "we know something of what goes on." * I realized here that we must get our photographs ready for the children to take home so that sharing will be natural, constant, and expanding between here and home.

* Easy to welcome such positive feedback. Important for us to encourage parents to understand that we need and value evidence of where things aren't going well with a child—if we are to matter.

Helen is learning adjectives and adverbs as easily as she learned nouns. The idea always precedes the word. She had signs for *small* and *large* long before I came to her . . . the other day I substituted the words *small* and *large* for these signs, and she at once adopted the words and discarded the signs.

—Ann Sullivan
from a letter to Perkins Institute
Helen Keller, *Story of My Life*

Time to Read

□ ■ □ ■ □ ■ □ ■ □ ■ □ ■ □ ■ □ ■ □ ■ □ ■ □ ■ □ ■ □ ■ □ ■ □ ■ □ ■ □ ■ □ ■

VISIT 8, MARCH 22 (Greg, Phillip, and Claire absent; Miss B. came to assist)

New Equipment

cardboard-covered looseleaf notebooks, one for each child, containing sample photographs of our activities to date—the illustrations in this book. Each page was enclosed in a plastic sheath to allow for much handling. The text used some phrases the children could already read and some new ones.

We couldn't come last week, but will be here twice this week. Miss B., another young member of our staff, came this morning.* She had been a great help in making the photograph books, so it was particularly appropriate for her to see the children's reactions, though Claire should have been here also to enjoy the delight her pictures produced.

* Miss B. was a recent graduate in Junior High Education —Science, who was a sort of apprentice in our Center.

Only the four little girls and Miss M. were in the cafeteria when we arrived. Miss B. and I joined them. Their
faces showed confusion and concern at first: "No Claire,
no visit last week?" We can only approximate the words.

I leaned over to greet someone and the long string of
blue beads I was wearing hung over the table. Each child
reached out to feel and hold them. (There is always more
individual notice when we are in the cafeteria setting,
away from the materials in the classroom.) When I came
near Lisa she held my hand and acted out: "You poor
thing, you have been sick." Our Lisa is the secretary for
sympathetic communications. Janie indicated by actions
that our visitor must have a name tag.

And now watch Brooke dignify and dramatize a new
and exciting event. With a ceremonious manner she took
both my hands and examined them with great care, then
reached for Miss M.'s left hand. With pride and anticipation of my pleasure she showed me Miss M.'s new engagement ring. The examination of my diamondless
hands—with timing for effect—was a dramatic prelude for
Brooke's announcement, and there was shared and palpable pleasure among us all in Brooke's striking way of
showing us the new diamond ring. Walking down the hall
Brooke held my unbejeweled hand in hers and I was comforted, as somehow I felt she intended me to be. Lisa es-
corted Miss B.

In the classroom I sat on the floor with the six closed
books in my lap and the four little girls came close. I held
up one of the books, cover toward them. By chance it was
Phillip's, saying "Phillip's Book" on the cover. Lisa immediately got to her knees and explained to me with gestures that Phillip was sick and then explained to Patty,
who had reached for it, that the book was not hers but
Phillip's. This annoyed Patty who could read names as
well as Lisa could.

The book slipped to the floor, opening as it fell, but resting closed. Four pairs of eyes had seen something of what was inside and eight hands grabbed for a copy from the pile, unscrambling whose was whose by the names on the covers.

I watched Patty. She opened to the first page which included the picture of the children around the tub blowing bubbles. Then she read with silent concentration running her finger under each sentence. "Patty is here, Greg is here," etc. She came to the word "and." Not knowing the word, she looked to me for explanation. Just once I touched Janie then Patty, saying "Janie *and* Patty." Patty got it immediately. So much for drill. She then went through the book, which so far did not contain many pages, reading names and words she knew and looking with delight. The decision to include the sentences they knew verbatim, and to vary these slightly, was justified. Everyone could find words he knew and devoured it all.

Janie was at my side suddenly and together we looked at and read from her book. Miss M. took Phillip's and immediately commented upon the effect the book would have in the school: "Around here *this* will impress them." (It is not by accident that no one in the school except Bobby's teacher has stepped in to see what goes on, and I suspect that Miss M. is under criticism or subtle harassment about us and about her university-sponsored program. We never heard a word about the school's reaction to the books.)

When Lisa saw the caption "Bubbles going up" under a bubble tube picture, she put the book down and pantomimed the bubble tube, tipping it from end to end with quite the proper space between her hands for that imaginary tube. Rather good oral reading, I thought, and in nice contrast to some of her early, meaningless mimicking.

We had to leave soon and Brooke was sad, almost wistful. We had brought no equipment, no Claire, and I guess she realized early that we were not planning to stay very long. (I remember my own beloved grandmother keeping her hat on during a visit long ago and my fearing she wouldn't stay long. I was afraid to ask and thus confirm my fear.) Miss B.'s notes about Lisa include:

> Lisa was independently interested in the books; first she looked at them with Janie and me and Janie wanted to point out something. Then Lisa saw the classroom rocking-boat in one of the pictures, showed it to me, but was concerned because in the picture it was upside-down and hence I might not recognize it. She grabbed Miss M., showed her the rocking-boat itself, and indicated that she should explain to me that these two were the same though in different positions. Miss M. did and Lisa was satisfied.

The books of photographs were certainly worth the effort. We have decided to continue the pictures and text for the children's simultaneous pleasure and learning. Bless the inventor of those plastic page covers. The children understandingly use their reading for communication and in the process must underline words with their fingers. No wonder they learn to read quickly! For them it is a breakthrough into the verbal world and exciting new dimensions—especially when coupled to their own concerns.

Summer Storms— and Questions

□ ■ □ ■ □ ■ □ ■ □ ■ □ ■ □ ■ □ ■ □ ■ □ ■ □ ■ □ ■ □ ■ □ ■ □ ■ □ ■ □ ■ □ ■

VISIT 9, MARCH 24

New Equipment

six envelopes of gels, each with a child's name printed on it and colored yarn attached so that it could be hung over the shoulder or tied around the waist. Each envelope contained six gels of different colors. These were listed on the outside of the envelope. On the edge of each gel was the name of its color.

marbles

dilution trays (plastic with many depressions—see pictures of this visit)

plastic eyedroppers

Claire begins:

When we came early today (two days after Mrs. H. and Miss B. were here) the children had just stepped off their bus. There were loud sounds of joy from Janie and Patty, or so I identified the sounds. All six were present and Brooke looked at me as if to say, "When Claire comes with armsful of stuff, it means that everything is going to be as it was before and people will stay a while." Mrs. H. first called the children to where she sat on the floor with her basket. She took out the six big envelopes of gels. No "Oh"s or "Ah"s as I had expected—rather, the children waited until each had his fat envelope in hand and all cer-

Colored Gels

What color is your
Gel, Patty?

Is it red or blue or
green or yellow?

Is it orange or
purple?

Yellow for Janie.

Blue for Brooke.

What color is your Gel, Lisa?

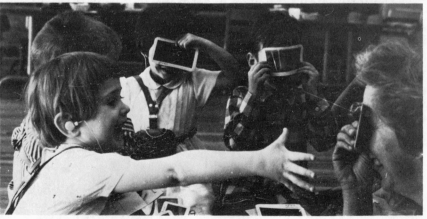

Janie wants her Gel.

Phillip looks through
yellow.

emoniously opened them at once to take out the gels. *Then* voice reactions came.

The packages themselves certainly took precedence over the contents for the first few minutes. Since we had been particularly careful in designing the envelopes so that they would be protective, carry meaningful descriptions of contents, and look attractive, this was reassuring not surprising. With delicate materials it is a good idea to arrange packaging which helps a child protect the objects, especially if he needs to carry them about. (Miss M. had mended those first gels with scotch tape until one could hardly see through them.)

Some years ago in a cooperative nursery school, I was surprised at the care which the children gave a rather delicate old gold-balance. I had brought it to school one rainy morning as a visiting piece of equipment, but the children's appreciation indicated that it should stay. The balance was stored on top of the piano to protect it from younger brothers and sisters and from the lower school of threes, these being fours. For some weeks it was used almost daily to weigh lightweight objects. The tweezers were a joy to the children and were managed with great dexterity to lift the graduated weights.

Unfortunately, this way of carefully handling precision instruments is stressed by certain schools of thought in using ordinary materials for which such care is superfluous and stifling. If children are hemmed in by an attitude of preciousness toward all classroom equipment, they tend to use all equipment only in the "proper" manner or simply don't use it at all. Chairs are indeed chairs, but they also make railroad trains, walls, or storefronts on occasion. (The gold-balance, of course, did not replace the sturdier and less complicated balances.)

A young child's interest in the new community of school and his wish to become a member of it request that we understand what is communicated *to him* by the ar-

rangement of a classroom, its materials, and their care—
lest we "organize" his thinking.

While the children explored the possibilities of six
gels apiece, I arranged the table for food color and the
new dilution trays.

Drops—of Water and Color

Brooke can put the
top on—

and take it off
to pour.

Blue drops.
Red drops.
Green, yellow,
purple, and
blue drops for
Janie, Brooke,
and Phillip.

Brooke shows
Claire a drop
of blue on the
dropper.

Claire writes:

I was curious about the way Mrs. Hawkins seated the children around the table for work with color in the dilution trays. She purposely seemed to break up the usual seating pattern (heretofore maintained by Miss M. for her work by taping each child's name to a place on the table). She answered my unasked question by talking to Miss M. about what she was doing. "With new activities there is an opportunity for grouping children in a different and possibly more advantageous way." I saw later that Lisa and Greg did very well together where Mrs. H. had provided for them. Brooke and Lisa would have been a trouble to each other.

The original use for those named places by which children could easily and naturally learn their own and each other's names had disappeared. They were long since experts at reading names, as is obvious throughout.

Claire notes my reasoning—that Brooke and Lisa would have annoyed each other. In addition, I was hoping that Lisa and Greg might make a new and interesting twosome. They did.

Greg and Lisa made such different trays of color! It took Greg a long time to figure out how to get color into his dropper, and Miss M. wanted to show him but laughingly said to Mrs. H., "I shouldn't show him, should I?"

We left Greg to go on dipping his dropper. Since this method carried only one drop of color at a time, the water in his tray took on particularly delicate variations in color. This pleased him for many minutes and gave the tiny wells of water quite a different density from Lisa's rather muddy mixtures which had much color squeezed into each. In about five minutes Greg exhibited his ability to learn in his own way and time by discovering how to squeeze the dropper, release it under water, and pull the colored liquid up into it. The expression of joy at his own discovery showed on his face and in his manner, and was

reflected in the faces of the three adults watching nearby.
Claire reports:

> Phillip was wrapped up in the joy of the colors them-
> selves. It seemed to me that he enjoyed the esthetic
> beauty of those little round drops of color more than the
> mechanics of his eyedropper. Lisa actually chortled over
> Greg's tray at one point·in obvious appreciation. She bab-
> bled to him in the longest stream of vocalization that I've
> ever heard from her. Then right at the end she and Greg
> laughed and laughed over something that was a mystery to
> us—but they shared it! I enjoyed seeing Greg laugh be-
> cause he usually just smiles, slowly, sweetly, and wist-
> fully.
> Mrs. H. averted a crisis when Brooke tried to use
> Patty's tray of colors. She told Brooke very seriously that
> she might squirt just one drop, not more, into Patty's tray. I
> didn't think Brooke could understand but apparently she
> did because she carefully squirted one drop and then
> turned back to her own tray. (Note for next time: We
> should have a jar of clean water in the middle so the chil-
> dren can rinse the droppers if they want to. The colors in
> most trays were muddy before long.)
> When wash-up time came the children loved cleaning
> the trays in the lavatory. It was almost as much fun to see
> the colors disappear rapidly down the white sink as to see
> them appear—or that is my guess.
> Almost as soon as Mrs. H. had taken the shakers from
> their basket, everyone was shaking and opening and spill-
> ing. Greg spilled first and looked up at Mrs. H. with fear.
> She laughed with him and helped him pick up, but he still
> must have felt troubled because when Phillip tried to help
> he just hit Phillip's hand hard.

I identify with Greg's fear of spilling accidents. The
standard treatment in my own childhood was a smack.
The sequence here is revealing and suggestive. Spill—
fear—no smack from adult—the smack by Greg to Phillip.
The fear in Greg was already coupled with past resent-
ment and currently came out in violence toward his best
and helping friend.

I watched Greg and Phillip soon afterward spend a long time with the shakers. They sorted and matched the contents of the plastic containers with the contents of the aluminum shakers—all this in an atmosphere of close, conspiratorial comradeship. Perhaps we had loosened that too close coupling of fear with violence by providing a climate in which accidents—even hitting your best friend when you don't mean to hurt him—do happen and can be overlooked.

> After a while I thought this activity had gone too far. Seeds, etc., were all over the floor and I felt that, in Mrs. H.'s words, things had deteriorated. She corroborated my judgment by suggesting we go a little early for milk.

The chaotic splendor of seeds, pods, rocks, and children can be imagined from Claire's pictures (page 70). Her concern for the deterioration taking place was valid. As I have indicated before, new teachers in our schools live in terror of such "disasters," first, because they are usually reprimanded by administrators for allowing them and secondly, because they have not learned how to use them well—or prevent them. Across-the-board disapproval ensures that those happy accidents, the potential stimulators of new ideas and ways of proceeding, will almost disappear. Fortunately, however, where young children live such accidents still happen in spite of the best laid plans. There was a time when I too feared the establishment and did not understand how to use chaos. The daily example of one teacher and one principal I was lucky enough to work under early in my teaching gave me courage to seek what was important though not approved, what was risky at times and not certain. Let me pass on some of that courage to neophytes.

Lest occasional chaos be confused with a monotonous pattern of falling apart, I want to continue for a moment. It is with this latter pattern that the well-intentioned reformer often confronts the usual authoritarian rule and thinks, no doubt, that a certain continuity-of-chaos improves upon the tedium and suffocation of authoritarianism. Often, too, it is the justifiable fear of continual chaos which supports the establishment in its rejection of messy innovation. Thus the possibilities for change are caught in a vicious circle.

The climate of a classroom is so often designed to be like a greenhouse where atmosphere, temperature, light, and air must be controlled to produce lettuces (or children) as undifferentiated as science makes possible. But children learn and think and send out new shoots in contact with rain, wind, sun, storm, and thunder. When one calculates that a child spends the crucial and central part of his waking day in school, it is obvious that the sterile, programmed hours of so many classrooms produce hothouse products in the most denigrating sense, and that such unlived lives, in Eric Fromm's words, do lead to violence.*

After several summer storms of our own today, Claire describes what happened after milk time.

> When I came back to the room I found Brooke trying to tie on her own envelope of gels. I helped her tie, then sat on the floor beside her. We took turns looking through the gels, and then I suddenly felt very uneasy with her. (See questions and discussion below.)

---

* What kind of abusive effect do schools have on children—when tensions and lack of substantive help impinge on teachers? As our knowledge of causes contributing to the battering of children grows, we understand that to help the child we must help the family. Unless we get help to teachers, our schoolchildren will continue to be "battered," though in more subtle if not less destructive ways. The syndrome is similar: *Certain children are at fault* and "invite" a sick parent's "reform" (beating, isolation, withholding of food, etc.). Our school establishment is more subtle—not different: *Certain Children are at fault* and invite a sick society's "reform": sedation, isolation, withholding of food, privilege, and approval. In such an atmosphere "learning problems" abound.

Waiting for the children when they returned from milk were colored glass marbles with the dilution trays instead of color and water. One marble would fit neatly into each depression. When Phillip dashed into the room and saw the marbles he grabbed one of the chairs (in a rough fashion for him) and sat down at the table with marbles and trays. He was very eager to start.

All the children clustered around that table. Janie turned her dilution tray upside-down and put marbles along the aisles between the bumps of the inverted tray. She was pleased with the new effect—with her ingenuity. So were we. One wonders whether her amusement at the substitution of marbles for water led her to substitute the bottom for the tray.

At the end of today's visit three "conspirators," Claire, Lisa, and Brooke, had a fine writing exercise on the floor by themselves with crayons and paper. They wrote their own names and others' and giggled together.

CLAIRE'S QUESTIONS AND A DISCUSSION OF THEM

When on the floor with Brooke I felt uneasy for two reasons:

1. I wondered whether we are perhaps reading too much into the children's reactions. Are they reacting less than we think they are? For example, I felt that Brooke was excited not as much by the gels *per se* but more because she was affected by the delight she saw on my face when she looked through the gels.

2. I also got an inkling of what it is to be a little bit afraid of children when you sense they have power over you. It was the way Brooke would ruthlessly push something away when she got bored with it and give you a look of superiority. It's an amazing thing when it happens for the first time, and I think this was the first time that I intuitively grasped that feeling. I'll have to talk about these questions with Mrs. H. They are hard to write about succinctly.

We did discuss these questions, at length. Let me try to sum up my reactions. Claire has pointed out two distinct aspects of the same phenomenon: a dynamic relationship between two persons, in this instance between an adult of twenty-two and a child of four (and she has properly questioned the communication between that child and a fifty-year-old).

She first asks if we are reading too much into the children's reaction to the materials and not enough into their response to us. Fair enough. Brooke most certainly reacted to Claire's presence as well as to the gels. What is not so clear, and what I think also occurs, is that Brooke responded to Claire's unstated desire *to keep Brooke involved in the gels*—to observe her.

Once Claire entered Brooke's circle Brooke's attention most certainly shifted from thing to person. At the end of the encounter Brooke left the scene, with her gels, and Claire felt abandoned. What happened in-between? Based on my knowledge of these two people and on my similar experience with children, including Brooke, let me hazard my understanding of the logic of this action and reaction.

Brooke's interest in the gels diminished as her concern with Claire increased. Any interest Claire had in the gels (which I suspect was minimal) diminished in some proportion to her increasing interest in Brooke's reactions and her wish to stimulate them. The shift in attention from the gels to each other was very rapid and dynamic. With the loss of the gels as a positive and meaningful focus for mutual attention, the relationship between Brooke and Claire deteriorated into a kind of power struggle.

In this arena Brooke was freer to act and thus had the upper hand. Sensing that she was becoming the forced object of Claire's observation and judgment, she simply walked away. (A teacher can learn to use this kind of personal relationship on occasion as a compass or altimeter, as another delicate instrument for measuring how matters stand between himself, a child, and material at hand, what direction to take, when to withdraw.) With a child like Brooke, the surest way for an adult to interfere with the child's interest in an inanimate object is to shift attention from the object to the child. Some children are less interested than others in adult reactions; they truly bestow their attention on the material at hand and keep it there with little effort.

Claire's fear of Brooke's power over her was the end of Claire's innocence with young children. Though different from adults, children are whole human beings, *and one manipulates or "plays" with them at the risk of being thrown overboard.* The power that children, especially children like Brooke, have over us is real. They are concerned with our thoughts and are not easily diverted. Their basic strength, as well as their weakness, lies in the direction of concern with personal relationships.

Brooke is already considered a threat to the narrow adult establishment for related reasons—she is perceptive and extremely critical. Miss M., who understands, likes, and appreciates something important about her, has recounted the reactions of other teachers in the school: "Brooke is too self-willed . . . She will have trouble."

Unfortunately for such children those rigid teachers who predict troubles are also in a position to make their prophecies self-fulfilling. On the positive side, I cannot believe that a mind as exciting as Brooke's—developing as it is in a world totally silent from birth—can be easily interfered with by those with smaller minds. But oh, their power and their narrow classrooms can make her miserable and sap her energy in constant battle.

Catastrophe Saves the Day

□ ■ □ ■ □ ■ □ ■ □ ■ □ ■ □ ■ □ ■ □ ■ □ ■ □ ■ □ ■ □ ■ □ ■ □ ■ □ ■ □ ■

VISIT 10, MARCH 31

New Equipment

box of large stainless steel bolts and nuts from a good junk yard

periscope prisms (the Army surplus variety)

playdough—made of salt, flour, and water and dyed with food colors

hard-boiled eggs and food color (for making Easter eggs)

paintbrushes and paper towels

plastic eggs with marshmallow bunnies and chickens inside. These were brought for Easter presents and were wrapped in tissue and nested in plastic berry baskets.

Today we brought in the first material for modeling—an individual packet of playdough for each child, each of a different pastel color. None of the five who chose the playdough was really engaged in the opening round; the children pressed it and looked at each other as though to say, "What is this for?" Patty joined in last, having spent a long time earlier with the periscope prism. She was very much amused as she explored the fact that one could see what was at the side by looking head-on. In her usual pattern she initially used the dough with more imagination than the others, who were uninvolved at first.

Claire's notes tell us:

> We haven't seen much of that kind of behavior lately. Brooke traded her own lavender-colored dough for Mrs. Hawkins's blue with a cunning little smile and a cautioning finger which seemed to say, "You have to take blue; I want yours." Lisa, more than she has lately, acted jealous of me and bid for my attention in a manner that was similar to Brooke's possessiveness of Mrs. Hawkins.

So, early this morning things were grinding away to a bored halt. I couldn't put my finger on the trouble. There was plenty of good stuff around, no pressures to use any one thing, but for some time nothing felt right or seemed exciting to any of us. Even with only six children, initiative is needed at such times and one searches: Why the sudden increase of possessive behavior in Lisa and Brooke? Was it linked to this particular morning's materials? With what happened last week? Yesterday's session here at school without us? Troubles at home for both or either little girl?

Miss M.'s recent and appreciative words echoed in my ears. "The children really look forward to your coming each week . . . they go to the reading board to ask whether you are coming on that day . . ." We know this may heighten tensions and rivalry, but why today specifically?

No certain answers to these questions came racing through my mind. But one tries to be flexible, tries not to push through a plan, but rather tunes in to small nuances which may be suggestive. It is hard to say how or whether such awareness is precisely responsible for a positive change, but a causal relationship can exist and suddenly things get started.

Greg is the center of this morning's getting off the ground, and, though I would not have predicted the time or materials which would spur his breakthrough, there have been indications. Over the weeks we have found him participating in more and more substantive ways, and in retrospect we have called this Greg's morning. His personal thrust affected us all. With the dough in some sense not being worth much, we shifted to egg-dyeing where Greg and catastrophe saved the day. (Watch how the dough becomes important later in the morning.)

In gathering equipment for today I did not foresee the importance of size in choosing containers to hold the dye, and hence the egg fitted too well as it slipped into the straight-sided plastic glass of color. What a piston this made! Colored water spurted from each child's glass over table and floor. Greg was ecstatic; pandemonium hung over us. Only the near impossibility of removing the eggs from their close-fitting sheaths saved that room from more explosions, rainbow fountains, and floods.

In Claire's words:

> . . . water everywhere, and it was almost impossible to get those eggs out. Here for the first time I understood what Mrs. H. has said about the lack of usable junk in a classroom. At first we couldn't find anything to substitute for the plastic glasses nor enough rags to sop up, and what *became* the glory of that egg-dyeing would have been lost if Mrs. H. hadn't been there. (Later we remembered the toy pots and pans, which were large enough for the eggs.)

Claire's panic is important to record. I wish our teachers didn't have to learn to "drive in traffic" before they understand the mechanics of what they are doing. A classroom stocked for emergencies (rags, paper, sponges, etc.) will not prevent them, nor, as by now it must be clear, does one want to prevent all of them, but emergency supplies encourage a teacher and children to make the most of accidents instead of panicking.

Out of the original chaos Greg's face, as he saw that his first egg had turned blue, is the thing to be remembered. He looked up with amazement and joy. Then when we had provided containers of a better shape he forgot us as he worked with precision and purpose to transform each of six eggs (and incidentally his two hands) from white to blue. Others played with color mixing and less exciting affairs; Greg had found what he had not known he was looking for—a kind of blue magic—and he didn't desert it. His own concentration saved him from my suggesting a conventional choice of several colors. Six blue eggs went home with Greg.*

At the end of the morning when Patty showed her mother a basket of predominantly orange eggs, she remarked that this was one of Patty's favorite colors. This suggests an answer to my query about Patty's apparent preference for delicately colored water for her tube while the others often get carried away with color-*adding*. It is as if Patty holds a color image in her mind and uses it as a guide. With no verbal communication one has to make tentative observations, building onto them as further clues emerge. I believe Patty selects and designs more than most of her peers—but, as we have observed, not in any rigid sense. Incidentally, Patty just became four this month. She is the youngest.

Claire adds:

Phillip was his usual quiet self with his eggs . . . totally absorbed. Greg's hands were completely blue but he did not panic this time as he has at such accidents in the past. Lisa sitting next to Greg was also very involved and didn't have a minute to look up. (See pictures of Lisa and Greg, page 140, which were made during this visit.)

* It is fun to speculate about Greg's staying with *blue*. Something for his future reference: Would *each* egg take the *same* color? Exploration of his freedom from teacher's suggestion? Sheer delight in *that* color?

When there was not a white egg left, we used the leftover dye for painting or dropping (in a Jackson Pollock mode) onto paper towels. The dye flows into the absorbent towels with an uncontrolled spreading effect. One intention here was to suggest to the children that there are new possibilities for old materials if one rethinks and recombines. (Chromatography captures an older group's concern.)

> Everyone took to coloring the towels, some gently and some very splashily. Lisa was in the latter category, putting lots of color on one towel. Phillip was cautious and gentle with his, watching and thinking about effects, and enjoying them.

By this time in the morning the early fogs of apprehension had lifted and we were out in the sun.

For Easter gifts I had brought pastel-colored plastic eggs of about actual egg size which opened in halves but stayed closed rather nicely. I thought that the neat opening and closing possibilities would please these dexterous hands. In each egg was enclosed a sugared marshmallow animal, to be popped immediately, I predicted, into mouths. "Never count your chicks . . ." Claire describes what a surprisingly magnificent gift the children made of these modest favors.

> The children's reactions to these were incredible . . . the excitement when they opened those eggs and found the animals! No one thought of eating or nibbling. Instead they just sat on the floor, opened their eggs, looked at the chicks and bunnies, laughed, made the throat sounds they do for pleasure, put the eggs together again, and laughed some more. This could have gone on for hours. Greg was amazing with his. He kept chortling and fondling his bunny and egg, and looked happier than I have ever seen him.

Brooke left the circle first and took her egg back to the playdough table. All followed, and out of the eggs came bunnies and in went playdough. Here also Greg continued to stay out of his own shell. He ran around with bunny in one hand and egg filled with playdough (color to match the egg) in the other.

At some point in what had become an Easter dance of color, shape, and movement, I sat at the table with the playdough and put enough of it inside one plastic egg to form an "egg" of the dough for my own amusement. When Greg noticed the dough facsimile it was almost too much for him. He dashed off into a far corner unable to contain his excitement. Brooke and Patty examined their eggs and rabbits through the prism, set them to nest nearby, then with Claire built tall towers of plastic strawberry baskets for the animals to live in.

Sufficient unto the day is the joy thereof!

"Such Science"

□ ■ □ ■ □ ■ □ ■ □ ■ □ ■ □ ■ □ ■ □ ■ □ ■ □ ■ □ ■ □ ■ □ ■ □ ■ □ ■ □ ■ □ ■ □ ■

VISIT 11, APRIL 14 (Miss M. absent)

New Equipment

long, flexible clear plastic tubing or hose

old alarm clock and old box cameras—to take apart

construction paper

colored chalk

large stainless steel shallow cake pan for wetting construction paper

balances—These were small wooden balances made by combining a sturdy base, a nail for fulcrum, and a yardstick into which holes had been drilled at even intervals. And unequal or equal arm balance could thus be made. Paper cups hung by pipe cleaners were used for balance cups. Styrofoam balls, paper clips, and all sorts of light-weight odds and ends were brought for weights.

Miss M. had been ill all week and the children had had a series of substitutes. (This morning it was Mrs. K.) In addition, we had brought with us our friend and visitor, Miss Weisskopf, from the Bank Street College in New York. All of these staff changes allowed us again to see the children with a new backdrop. Claire and Miss W. joined the children and Mrs. K. in the cafeteria while I set out our equipment.

Greg and Phillip must have gulped their milk this morning. They raced into the room while I was still arranging things and by the time other faces appeared the boys were blowing vigorously through the new lengths of clear flexible tubing. I had thought of the tubing as supplementary to water play, but Phillip and Greg wanted no such narrow grooving when there was new material to be investigated. To see how the boys were blowing and feeling the air at long distance suggested that such a magnifier of sound might be very useful with these deaf children. (String telephones, which are great fun, are rather useless unless one hears.) The picture of Janie blowing, taken on this day, appears in Appendix 2 (page 138) and shows her own invention for blowing at or speaking to herself.

The four little girls came in with a certain pride, flanked as they were by two big ones: Claire and Miss W. (Anyone who knows fours and fives has seen how they válue a chance to be with youth.)

Mrs. K., the substitute teacher, carefully observed all morning and left Miss M. a note which included: "I have never spent such an interesting day; I wish more deaf children could have such science." Well, we do too, [and it was kind of Miss M. to share the note with us.]

As I watched the children's intensity in investigating the old alarm clock and some old box cameras with Miss W., I realized that we need more for these children to use their clever fingers on. They were greedy to take things apart, turn winders, etc. Phillip and Greg, however, stayed with their long plastic tubes, now filled with water, and weren't interested in anything else for a long spell. They blew and blew bubbles at long distance and were convulsed with laughter at the effect. Lisa got a turn, and I tried to wash the end of the tubes with soap occasionally to cleanse my hygienic conscience.

Drawing with Chalk on Wet Paper

Purple and red
chalk on Patty's
blue paper
make a picture.

While Lisa is already
drawing, Phillip rolls up
his sleeves.

After last week's reaction to spreading color on paper towels, I was interested in trying another kind of paper which other children have enjoyed. (Our once-a-week visit rushes us into some new phase each session and I do not recommend the pace.) Chalk on wet paper makes strange effects. We borrowed from the kitchen a large flat pan to submerge the construction paper in and the children managed their own dipping after one demonstration. Once they saw the construction paper's dull finish transformed by the water into a bright surface, they were ready to go. Then the flowing quality of the chalk on watered paper increased their anxiety for a turn—and another and another.

I have wondered at the special delight one sees when children behold something known (here construction paper) in a changed condition. It is a different reaction, I believe, from that given to a totally new phenomenon, but I can't say just how it differs. Does it have to do with the surprise at seeing an old acquaintance transformed? Perhaps at such times we approach some natural spring from which a child drinks in his own brand of learning and his developing recognition of likeness and difference, of change and the lack of it.

Brooke, who had been wandering about, was particularly caught in admiration for the flow of chalk on wet paper. She slowly covered a yellow sheet with blue chalk, watching each stroke in the way that we sometimes unself-consciously lose ourselves in observing our own actions. Claire watched her.

> Brooke glowed with pleasure when she showed me one of her drawings. She made lots and lots of different ones. Toward the end of the morning she drew a lovely circle of black in the middle of a sheet of paper and filled the circle with orange and blue. This last was quite different from her others.

Brooke was long at it—not just testing and going off. Chalk in hand felt right to her. I may be wrong, of course, but I think that reading and writing will transform Brooke particularly. She lives in such a private world and reminds me sometimes of a princess in a tower who will be rescued—but only by her true love, not yet known.

When I set things up this morning it was my intention to protect the children's introduction to the two simple balances by putting them at side stage. I wanted to introduce them, not head-on, but tangentially and in sequence with enough surefire old stuff so that the children would not rush all at once to the balances just *because* they were new. Such structuring has at least two justifications: it allows a child sufficient time to use a new piece of equipment without having at once to share or wait turns. Materials such as this yardstick-*cum*-weights-on-upright are more likely to speak to a child when there is time for continued experimentation.

In addition, a lentissimo approach provides a teacher the luxury of observation with a kind of time-lapse sequence. If a child is not under pressure to make the most of his allotted time and if he finds the materials worth his attention, then one *may* observe in reflected behavior the "borning" of new ideas—not an everyday privilege since ideas emerge so rapidly and are so subtly hidden. Something of this we caught with camera and eye around the balances.

At one point Brooke had followed me from the wet paper to the balances. She was not faintly interested, though she watched me make one of the arms of the yardstick move by dropping a large paper clip into a cup. She held in her mind's eye, I surmise, her marvelous creations of chalk and in no sense even *saw* the balance.

Some of us believe that to tamper with a child's already deeply bestowed attention is to court trouble. One can minimize this with a speaking and hearing child, but the silence of the deaf induces endless brazen interference. Brooke, as we have observed, has pitched her will against such attempts. Patty and Janie manage in a less head-on way.

I keep an early picture of Brooke in mind as a paradigm of communication about these matters. She once

turned to me as she left a situation in which I was bidding
for her attention with small blocks and give me a grin
with a finger shake, mischievousness just hidden. She
seemed to say, "I am finished with those matters you still
offer and now I must get on with my own affairs." If important moments are to count, I believe the directive is
clear. We must sharpen our skills for observing the out-
ward evidence of inner involvement—of that logic of behavior—so that, as teachers, we can build upon it not tear
it down.

Brooke walked away from the balances; Patty and
Phillip stayed. The picture of Phillip tells his story; words
are superfluous. Patty tried again and again to keep the
yardstick horizontal by holding it and then very carefully

It balances.

removing her hands. It was such a privileged view into how she approaches a new experience. No hurry, no belief on faith or on one or two testings, but the careful observation, trying, and thinking which then lead her into such off-beat and fresh parts of the forest.

Mrs. K. watched Greg with a balance and remarked that he seemed to be getting the idea of it. Perhaps in her sense he was. In fact, there are so many ideas related to balance that one tries to avoid closure. Claire captures Greg's more dramatic and deep concerns.

> Greg made a spider out of his styrofoam ball and some pipe cleaners, then hung it on the balance by one "leg." A beautiful little scene occurred when he threw the spider at Janie and Patty who had been watching him, still in their long smocks for chalk-drawing. They clutched each other in mock horror and fear . . . not sure whether they were scared or not. When they backed off from the spider, however, they dissolved in giggles and laughter.

With the quick action typical of all these young actors, Greg left the scene to Patty and Janie, one balance to each. For the next few minutes every time I noticed the two girls they were both engrossed in using various light weights to tip the balance arms—first to one side then to the other.

At the end of the morning I saw Janie's mother peeking through the tiny window of the back door. She came in and reported to me that she had been watching the two girls for twenty minutes and was amazed at their persistent work with the balances. So, indeed, was I.

> Brooke went to the water pool from the balance but left almost at once and returned to the chalk and wet paper. Lisa stayed at the pool alone for a time, working very hard to fill a long tube with water, using the funnel.
> She paid no attention to anyone or anything else!
> Greg loved the old clock which still has a workable

Balance

Will one large paper clip
send the high end down?
Patty will try it and see.

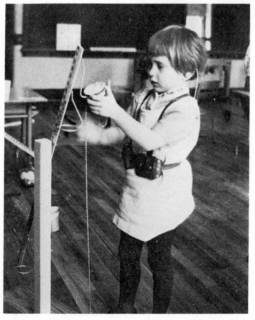

The chain is long and
heavy. When Janie
gets the chain inside
the cup—then down
will go the other arm
of the balance.

alarm. When he wound it and got it to ring he carried it around and tried to put it to everyone's ear. Janie and Patty were not the least interested. They were busy with the balances. Greg seemed to be a completely different child today. He was more aggressive, more fun-filled, *and more vocal.* At one point he carried around the yardstick from the balance, making motions as if to hit with it. Mrs. H. told him it was not for hitting, but said he could carry it around for as long as he wished. He did, understanding her completely, and he was not at all crushed.

When it was time to put things away Janie and Patty had a marvelous time fitting all of the balance stuff into the two cigar boxes we used for storage. They divided up the pipe cleaners, paper clips, styrofoam, etc., in two rows and then packed them in piece by piece.*

Everybody stayed busy. Brooke returned to the water pool and blew bubbles in a new, more sustained way, then again went back to the chalk and paper to make more drawings.

We stopped in time to have a leisurely clean-up and everyone helped with good spirits. Miss W. and I tried to find and put those tiny screws back in the cameras without much success. Mrs. H. hopes we can invent something better to use with screws for next time.

* By providing only lightweight "junk" to be used with such a balance it can be better exploited. See Appendix 2 for further balance information.

Patty's Game

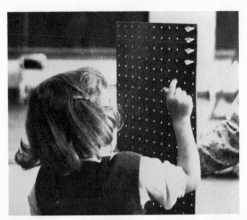

1.
1 peg
2 pegs
3 pegs
4
and many
holes.

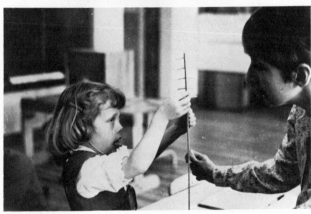

2.
1, 2, 3, 4, 5 pegs
and still many holes.

3. Many many pegs and no holes.

Children, when they construct things in play, normally play after the eolithic fashion: a pointed board suggests the making of a boat, and if the toy, in process of construction, begins to look less and less like a boat, it can conveniently be turned into an airplane. Select the child who appears most ingenious in the making of this class of toys, present him with adequate tools and lumber, give him a simple plan which must, however, be adhered to until completion, and usually his ingenuity gives way to a disheartening dullness. Poor children usually do not have this kind of opportunity, and it is notorious that poor children make themselves the best playthings. They have to make them out of scraps, and the scraps constitute variety. They are eolithic craftsmen; it is not only that eolithic craftsmanship can get along without uniform material and plans—it is precisely the non-uniformity of scraps and the absence of set plans which form the circumstances for its best development.

—Hans Otto Storm, "Eolithism and Design,"
Colorado Quarterly, Winter 1953.

Forbidden Games Start a Good Day

□ ■ □ ■ □ ■ □ ■ □ ■ □ ■ □ ■ □ ■ □ ■ □ ■ □ ■ □ ■ □ ■ □ ■ □ ■

VISIT 12, APRIL 21 (All present. Lisa, though, was ill upstairs and went home early.)

New Equipment

our invention: pieces of pegboard (one with hinges attached); square wood rods 1 inch x 1 inch, one to two feet long, drilled on all four sides with holes at intervals to match pegboard holes; nuts and bolts which fitted holes in pegboard and rods; golf tees which also fitted holes in pegboard.

screwdrivers

plastic two-gallon jugs

This was a morning of tightly packed action and innovation, a morning in which the children showed their growing sureness of touch, selection, and transformation of simple materials for *their own* needs and understanding. In only two short hours with five children we were as usual unable even to see, let alone record, a fraction of the action. Claire's pictures are invaluable in helping to read between the lines of these notes.

The action began with a glorious to-do about water in the nearby girls' lavatory. Our pedestrian aim was to fill the two-gallon carriers. But once we had hitched the clear plastic hose to the faucets, turned on the tap, and watched the water make its bubbling, halting way up, down, around, and through the six feet of transparent hose into the carrier, we were fascinated by the process—the children and I.

We were all so absorbed in watching the water and bubbles travel through the clear hose that the two-hole plastic jug overflowed with a fountain of water. No one rushed to turn off the faucet. The overflow fountain caused little trouble in that old lavatory with its big open drain in the middle of the cement floor, probably never before used in all of its seventy years for a sanctioned fountain. With time, privacy, and primitive plumbing on our side, we were able to savor forbidden games for a nice long spell before we carried the dripping jug back to the classroom. Phillip, who had finally released the hose from the faucet at my request, carried it proudly back to the room, went to the water pool, and threw it in with giddy abandon—a waterman home from the lake.

Claire tells how our invention was used.

Brooke was the first to notice and go to the new building materials: pegboards, rods, and bolts which Mrs. H. had put out on the floor in a far corner of the room; but once this new stuff was discovered everyone joined the exploration. Mrs. H. tried to get Phillip and Greg to try something else first, but no luck. Fortunately we had made enough to go around for a first try. Brooke showed amazing dexterity in screwing the bolts into the pegboard holes. Patty was the first to discover that one could fasten two pieces of pegboard together with a wooden rod as connector. Then everyone busily screwed and tugged and put on nuts. All worked very hard this morning. I saw Janie discover how a nut is used to secure a bolt and try it for her first time. She and Patty watched carefully to see the bolt come out the far side of the hole as Janie turned the screwdriver.

Just once Janie returned to the balance, her preoccupation of last week. The boards and bolts must have crowded out other possibilities because she spent most of the morning building with them. When we were cleaning up and putting away at the end of the morning Janie helped pack the nuts and bolts. Then she left and walked over to the balance. She looked at it with a sort of regret that one couldn't manage two such enterprises in a given time.

During the morning Patty found the box of golf tees which I had brought as a possible alternative to bolts for use with the pegboards. As she and Greg discovered, tees, with their tapered stems, fit into the holes very securely. Then there arose a nice problem. Unless one held the pegboard above the floor or table the tee would not go in completely.

Each of the children dealt with this restriction in his own way. Greg put in four bolts at the corners to serve as risers that enabled him to put the tees in the elevated pegboard. Patty, who might have copied had she not been Patty, took her board to Miss M., requested her to hold it at a certain angle, and proceeded to fit peg to hole in an obviously careful sequence. Miss M. tried to put one tee in (the temptation is irresistible), but Patty indicated sternly that Miss M. really did not know how to play this particular game according to Patty's rules, and that there was no time to explain.

With delight Phillip found the small hinges we had attached to a rectangle of pegboard. He examined the folding and opening of the hinges in his quiet way, and again I restrained myself from working with this little boy.

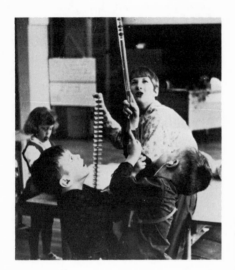

Water in Tubes

1. Greg and Phillip used a very long plastic tube one morning. They put in water and marbles, but left enough air for a big bubble. Down-down-down the marbles wobble . . .

2. and up goes the bubble—fast, when Phillip and Greg hold the tube straight . . . fast jump the marbles through the bubble . . . sometimes those marbles break the bubble into two or three.

Though Phillip is wary of adult interference and withdraws when advice is needlessly offered, he *can* ask for help. Most often he very competently uses his own compass for self-guidance.

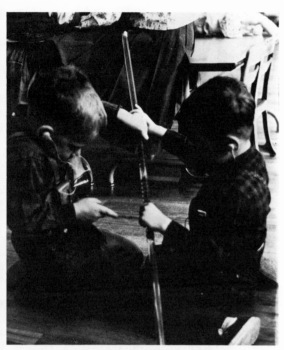

3. Sometimes the boys want to make the bubble go very slowly. They tip the tube, and almost make the bubble stop.

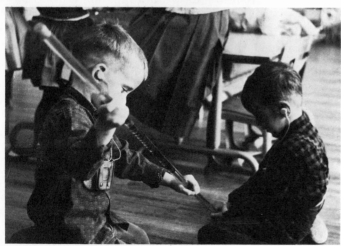

4. Again they turn the tube . . .

and again

and again . . .

and again.

Claire's notes continue:

Greg and Phillip made the most marvelous "invention." Together they chose the longest tube (four feet), corked one end securely, filled it with water cup by cup through the funnel, added as many marbles as they could capture, left a three-inch bubble, and corked the top tightly. As they raised one end of the tube and then the other they chortled at the effect on the marbles as they went through the bubble. With their four hands and no squabbling they kept tipping the tube from end to end. Much busy peace in the room. Patty was still working with the golf tees; Janie, after forty-five minutes, was still working on her "house," using boards and bolts; even Brooke had settled down at the water pool with many small plastic pill containers and their close-fitting tops. She found the new plastic cigar box and packed it carefully with the small pill containers, each full of water.

The peace and the activity held. It was good to see Brooke so involved. Janie's persistence and adeptness with the building stuff were a marvel to watch and a joy to assist. When she tackles a project she supplies enough of her own design to maintain self-direction. She accepts only minor help which furthers her own plans.

When Patty had finished her number game with the golf tees she went to investigate Janie's affairs. Janie, who was studying the door-with-hinges, showed it to Patty and insisted that Patty see that the hinges would open and close in only one direction. Patty was impressed, and assured Janie that she appreciated the properties of those hinges.

One is reminded here of the special language which some hearing twins invent for their own communication before they learn to speak their native tongue. Patty and Janie have their own almost invisible and certainly inaudible language. But here I want to consider the implications of this short interplay for a moment in relation to

Janie's House

Janie made a house one day. She used bolts and nuts and pegboards and wood and the big screwdriver. Janie worked and worked.

Janie was still putting on the roof when Patty moved in. The little cash register came with Patty—to furnish the house that Janie built.

communication skills and materials. Remember that these four-year-olds have essentially no spoken language. (Patty has none; Janie's very few words she uses on occasion, but not with Patty.) The materials they "discussed" here fall into the general category of blocks (bricks). Their value for stimulating communication is underlined: being open-ended and not designed for one answer (in contrast, say, to puzzles), they stimulated Janie to tell Patty something quite subtle that *she* had discovered *about* them. The value of this experience, for both children, is obvious. As my good friend and associate Bill Hull says about some materials, "They have a manageable complexity." Here the children wished to discuss some such quality.

First things first in this early world. After the matter of how the hinges worked was clear and before the door was hung and the roof raised, Janie invited Patty to move into the house. Patty first dashed off with great purpose to find something. Janie went back to work and Patty returned with a small cash register she had taken from Miss M.'s desk "to furnish the house with." In went the cash register, in squeezed Patty (resembling the rapidly growing Alice after she drank out of that first bottle labeled "Drink me"). Patty's fingers pounded at the tin cash register and she could just turn her cramped head to grin out the window. Claire adds details:

> Patty was in the house now. Janie found a roof for the top but then Patty didn't fit; so while Patty stayed in Janie built the four roof supports higher. Such dear friends they are, no squabbling—just sharing and working together.
>
> A little trouble with one of the empty plastic tubes and marbles. Greg and Phillip were rolling marbles down the tube and catching them, when four escaped and Brooke retrieved them. Did she return them to Greg and Phillip? Of course not. She tormented the boys until Greg changed course by putting his remaining marbles in one of the

large plastic water carriers and ran around the room shaking it. The noise was glorious and the vibrations palpable. The two boys had made a new game where Brooke was chasing *them* to have a turn.

If someone had told me the first time I came here that Greg and Phillip would act as they did today, I wouldn't have believed it—Greg running around laughing, calling attention to himself, playing for so long with Phillip with no self-consciousness and no deterioration in the play. Another whole side of both boys is emerging.

Late this morning about fifteen high-heeled ladies came into the classroom to observe. (They were visitors at Fillmore from a city university.) The kids were so busy they hardly noticed the adults.

The ladies were with us for the last fifteen minutes. They wandered about and watched but became invisible in the atmosphere which the children had woven around their own affairs. My remaining impression of these visitors is that when they first filed in they were giantesses. This is the trick one's own consciousness plays with scale, exaggerated here, I suppose, by my spending a good part of the time sitting on the floor or stooping and by my own professional sheath of separation from the outer world while in school.

Brooke underlined again today how much diversity is required if all children are to flourish. The morning had been about par for her, suggesting to me that she had not gotten enough out of it. I know she needs a one-to-one relationship more than the others do. So at the end of this morning I invited her to help carry our junk to the car. Fortunately her ride home was late and she and I had a good half-hour together.

We made more trips than necessary so that Brooke, who was very much pleased, could have more time to help. On our first trip my car had to be unlocked. Reaching for the keys, Brooke immediately elected herself to

ceremoniously unlock both doors and trunk. She wanted
to know what each key was for, but my house key presented a mystery still to be explained. Different keys,
different locks, unaccustomed hands, but much determination resulted in stowed gear and a glowing Brooke.
Bursting with responsibility she locked up at last and we
went for another load. After three trips we were back in
the classroom where the adept locksmith absolutely refused to return my keys.

With that challenging grin on her face she confronted
me from across the room, keys in hand. With the Brookes
of this world (when danger is not at issue) I refuse to
break such an impass by using authority or by running
faster. (These must be reserved as good coinage when
avoiding danger.) I have face to save—not rank to pull,
which in a situation of this kind is not playing the game.
So I borrowed from Greg's ingenuity and started another
game.

I turned my back to Brooke and stooped to draw a car
with doors on the blackboard. Before I could finish the
sparse outline Brooke was beside me watching. Next to
the car I drew a house with a door and in it a large key-
hole. Still holding my keys she selected the car keys,
"opened" the sketched car door, the trunk, and then
shifted to my house key for the house door. She tried it
again and again with laughter, gave me the keys unasked
and tried to draw her own house beside mine.

She reborrowed my keys to use on her drawing, and
then while my back was turned was picked up to go
home. For one sinking moment I thought she had taken
those beloved keys with her, but after a short hunt I found
them on the window sill. Luck and Brooke had not failed
me.

NOTE FOR NEXT VISIT

The pegboard with bolts is great for some and would be frustrating for others *if* they were expected to use it in any specified way or time, or if there were not enough other kinds of equipment at hand. The dexterity which the screwdriver requires is challenging to Janie and Patty, too annoying for Greg (he substituted fingers), and not interesting for Brooke. So it is with most good stuff. It speaks to children at one time or another but not always when or how one expects it to. Will try shorter screwdrivers next time. In a classroom not permitted hammers, wood, and nails, could these pinch-hit? See pages 140 and 142 for additional pictures of the children using today's equipment.

Changes Noted—
Summing Up

□ ■ □ ■ □ ■ □ ■ □ ■ □ ■ □ ■ □ ■ □ ■ □ ■ □ ■ □ ■ □ ■ □ ■ □ ■ □ ■ □ ■

VISIT 13, APRIL 28

New Equipment

pulleys
stubby screwdrivers to replace the long ones

Before the children themselves come into focus today, I want to speak of the change that has been evident and to indicate that at the end of this morning, my last visit, a preface is finishing. It is a preface which the children's use of these weeks has defined. Until last week I had not felt there was enough information to hazard a prediction or a summation—the former being based on the latter—for these six children.

We have been concerned with short-term, week-to-week plans which would provide involvement for the children and feedback for our understanding of how they individually used the materials and the climate we provided. Until one has some experience in observing how a given child structures his learning in a *variety* of situations—how he ticks—it is presumptuous to predict or to set any long-range plans. Even then, of course, plans and predictions for the young are subject to sudden shifts,

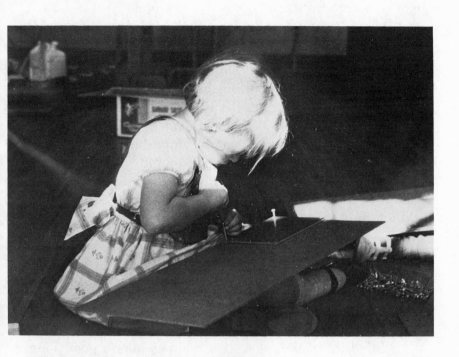

Screwdrivers

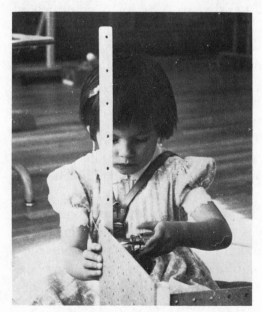

The end of the screw-
driver just fits into
the slot of the bolt
and helps Brooke and
Janie turn the bolts.

more with certain fours than others since in some human beings patterns jell earlier than in others.

Our not seeing these children in out-of-school situations, even on the school bus or with other children on a playground, has been a limiting factor in our understanding of each as a whole human being, and has accounted for a certain truncation, opportunistic modes of structuring the mornings, and a too rapid variation in materials. I have had to speed my own attempts to understand by introducing a variety of classroom situations in which to observe the children. At the end of this chapter there are sketches of the kind I would make were I planning for their subsequent school months.

This morning a slower tempo pervaded in contrast to last week's intensity, and though this change of mood was in part planned, it was so planned as a response to what I judged the children had indicated as a sequential step.

With Lisa back and well, I want to take a good long look at her. I watched her first at a physically complicated task she had set for herself. In one hand she held a clear plastic jar, and in the other she clutched some marbles. Now the fist of a plump four-year-old will not hold much, nor is it very dexterous while trying to hold on to things. Lisa dropped and retrieved more than one marble in what I took to be her attempt simply to fill the jar. She managed with skill and serenity to retrieve the roll-aways and put them into the plastic jar. Almost by magic she produced the snap-on top (where had she hidden *that?*), capped the jar, raised it to her ear, and then gave it a shake with a wide smile of self-congratulation on her face. Only then did I realize that it was a "shaker" she had designed and made for herself. None that we had put together held marbles. Had she combined two ideas: the long water tubes of marbles which she saw before going home sick last week and the shakers without water?

It will be remembered that we did not find much of significance in the use of those shakers when we introduced them in Visit 7. That Lisa stored away the idea for future use and was able to introduce a variation on the theme gives us a useful bit of insight into her use of old stuff in self-designed ways and of her growth.

I kept the close-up on Lisa, in the classroom, relishing the fact that this was possible without her interacting with my attention. She is changing and shedding the need for constant ratification. Later in the morning, then, I watched her working to fill one of the long bubble tubes with water. Because of her shortness, the length of the tube she had chosen, and hence the angle to which she had to tip it to get water from her container to the tube's opening, Lisa poured more water on the floor than in the tube. She had already corked the far end of the tube and inserted a funnel in the opening (useful in the past with shorter tubes); but the funnel here added to her trouble with its wide angle slope when tipped.

After an interminable time, to this observer, when the water level did not rise in the tube and there was a river on the floor, Lisa gave up momentarily and found her own solution. She climbed onto a chair (both hands full, having refilled her can with water from the pool), looked *down* into a now perpendicularly held funnel and tube, and poured the whole can of water in slowly to prevent overflow! I missed seeing how she managed to cork the top end, but my next view of Lisa showed her using her long, well-corked bubble tube with expertness and appreciation.

Had she carried in her memory from weeks ago Brooke's similar use of a chair; or did she have in her mind's eye the photograph and accompanying description of it? That picture went home in the photo book. We cannot know, but it was reassuring to see her again solve a complicated problem she set for herself, selecting and discarding from her environment instead of asking for help. Claire's notes catch Lisa in another episode.

> Brooke and Lisa worked together with a long empty plastic tube—using it for an inclined plane. They kept dropping marbles down it and watched them scoot across the floor; then one or the other would run after the marbles and bring back a handful—no friction at all—none between the children and little between marbles, tube, and floor.
>
> Janie was using a stubby screwdriver with the boards and bolts. Not so sure this is any easier than the longer one. We should bring both next time so that the children can choose.

Claire is right. We should have brought both. I had thought that the short screwdrivers might be easier to use. Not necessarily so. If a child was interested and able, as Janie was, the long one worked well, and for those who could not yet manage the long ones, the short ones were not much better. It was more a matter of the coordination needed for turning than the length of the tool.

Claire noticed:

> Phillip was very helpful to Lisa at the water pool. He helped her fill a squeeze bottle with water so that she could then squeeze that water into a bubble tube. As their pictures show, they were having a great time together. (Another way to fill a tube!)
>
> Miss M. told me an interesting thing about Lisa. Her mother reported that her Sunday School teacher had asked where Lisa had learned the written names of colors as well as how to identify them. Lisa's mother had answered, "Not at home," and then had asked Miss M. about it. Miss M. was certain it was the gels with the names of their colors printed on them. I realized from this episode that Lisa had taught herself by playing with the gels without our fussing over her. This is one way, as F. H. has suggested, that children teach themselves to read.

More Pulleys—More Water

To make a small
pulley-stand
Janie uses bolts
and sticks,
and works very
carefully.

Phillip squeezes water into Lisa's plastic
bottle so that Lisa can fill her long tube.

Brooke worked hard and was satisfied with a little right angle structure she made of boards and bolts. It stood nicely as a tent.

With Janie I went through a long, laborious task using bolts and was amazed at her dexterity, perseverance, and enthusiasm. She was trying to attach a piece of pegboard onto a 1 inch x 1 inch x 18 inch stick. It was arranged so that the screw had to be turned in an awkward manner with tiny motions. She never gave up even when I felt like swearing at the board. Then just as we were about to see the bolt peek through so that we could put on the nut, all the children were taken out for "class pictures." I felt a great letdown.

When the children returned I was still tying a pulley onto the jungle gym; the pictures of Patty and Janie using the pulley on pages 124 and 125 tell that story. Claire describes the end of the day:

Phillip and Greg, who had returned from an ear test, didn't want to stop playing with the tubes and marbles. They were using the long tube for an inclined plane as Lisa and Brooke had done. Their friendship seems stronger. Was it strengthened by their making the bubble tube with marbles last time?

The pulley was great fun but things got a little out of hand after a while.

Things get out of hand for many reasons with the youngest children. Here I felt it had to do with the fact that our morning was chopped up and interfered with by a series of interruptions. We have usually been happily free of this. The children, I submit, resented this shortening of their time in the classroom and simply were not ready to leave when the clock hit 10:30.

Their behavior is classic, of course, for children pulled away prematurely from engaging work. Short as our visits have been, I have started clean-up early enough to avoid trouble, thus making it a part of the whole. But this morning I too felt cheated of the time needed to fully explore with the children.

Claire came alone for the last visit to Fillmore. We might have called it her "Final." Her brief notes indicate how things went:

> Greg was a changed boy again (from the first time I met him) . . . Lisa was more settled down . . . It was a busy morning and the time flew. I enjoyed it.

The documentary of what Claire has observed and learned over these weeks is in her photographs. Once she had conquered the technicalities of taking pictures of those rapidly moving young ones she turned her attention to photographing the essence of what she saw. The sequential record of how the children were involved makes a living record of these weeks. What significance this visual history had for the children will be remembered from our earlier descriptions. To me, for whom both young teachers and children are my class, the photographs are testimony of the learning that took place.

Had circumstances and time permitted us to continue with these children, we would at this point be shifting emphasis from soundings and foundations to structures. I underline *emphasis* since we know that work with the young is seldom far away from the opening of new doors. New and old foundations and the structures built on them have a way of emerging concurrently when things go well in the lives of children, or of fortunate adults. The precise time of shift in emphasis will differ for each of these six. It is to spell out some of these differences that teachers take time to make notes, thus adding to their own insight into each child's future and their ability to plan for it.

I begin with *Brooke*—let us say for alphabetical reasons. She certainly has "that within which passeth show." Both to Miss M. and to me Brooke makes sense in her individual manner of structuring the school world for her learning. It takes skill to provide the order she requires. In her contacts with other adults at school she is a threat. "That one must learn to obey," a coordinating teacher said to me one morning in the cafeteria. Miss M. reported that Brooke was often in trouble with the music (rhythm) teacher because she would leave the scene when bored. I do not deny that her mode of operating, her hearing loss which I suspect is greater than the others', but primarily her astute critical sense require extra work and under-

To Make a Pulley

1. Patty tied one end of a string to the plastic water carrier, put the other end over the pulley wheel—

2. and pulled—

3. and pulled—

standing on the part of a teacher. If prized, however, her unique approach adds sure excitement to the whole relationship between this child, her teacher, and subject matter.

Brooke is a fighter, and when such a one turns her energy toward self-transformation and learning about the world this is not a minor advantage. She is alert to nonsense and to roads of no significance for herself; she could not have become such a complex and fascinating child, with such a magnificent sense of humor, had she not refused to allow herself to be manipulated. She is reading already in the best sense of the word for a four-year-old—when and if she needs to—and, being deaf and being Brooke, she needs written language in order to communicate the subtle insights of her own mind. She is the least verbal physically of the six yet she is the most ex-

4. and pulled—

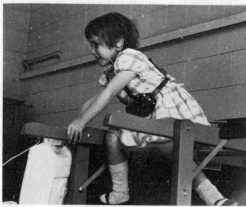

5. until Janie, sitting high on top of the jungle gym, could reach that water carrier.

pressive in figurative or imaginative ways. It is Brooke who most often has abstract ideas to communicate. With her tough, inventive mind she will teach herself to read well by almost any method a teacher offers—unless she is unlucky enough to get a teacher who tries to "break that will." Even then I am betting on her to carry on a good fight.

But what do I see as an optimal setting for Brooke? One which goes much faster initially in using the printed word. Because reading-language has been taught here in a group, Brooke has not been able to go as fast as her need and readiness would allow. As noted, she learns most rapidly in a one-to-one communicating relationship with or without words. Brooke, more than any of the others, has been and will be released by the coupling of the written word with the thing, activity, or action. She bestows her best attention upon materials which are offered with words. (See page 114 with keys and drawings.)

If the school world makes sense to her, the daydreaming and withdrawal will be minimized—and the reverse is certainly true. What a challenge awaits the teacher who can and will take the time to observe and learn with this one! We have not been of enough help to Brooke. I am just beginning to understand how she functions and it is hard to leave her at this point.

Because the self-regulating *Phillip* lives in such a different part of the forest I want to think about him next, in contrast to Brooke. For Phillip the printed word is not yet much needed or of much use. It will be if well integrated with his primary concerns: exploring the physical world, admiring its phenomena, and insatiably observing and experimenting.

If reading and writing are pushed at him before he sees how they fit his needs, his defenses of boredom and daydreaming will be called up against what is still irrelevant for him, *and his learning slowed.* Just as we have seen him teach himself with open-ended materials, so he will, if not forced, make the printed word his own. Boys like Phillip succeed under their own banners and fail only when squeezed into a rigid time scale or narrow method during early and vulnerable times in their lives. Who does not understand these basic truths? Only those who, by not providing "raw" materials, rule out the setting in which the Phillips exemplify how learning proceeds for them, how much they can teach and how well pace themselves.

Lisa will be using the printed word easily from here on, but seeing her employ newly released energies for inventive and self-guided pursuits suggests that she should not be rushed into reading and writing. She will have little trouble there but her compulsive habits of trying to please and imitate are too recently set aside. She will bring a deeper and subtler understanding to the written word if she is not skipped to the symbol until she has grasped enough reality to make it meaningful.

She needs more time for expansion—for stretching her new muscles of freedom—freedom from the need for constant approval. The psychic energy which she earlier spent in searching for people's reactions and then in manipulating them is being released for growth and exploration of a wider world. Our particular role cannot be accurately defined in this development, but I believe it is a positive one. Her recent behavior suggests that she has used our visits and materials well.

Patty is expanding daily into a world of her own structuring. She was already moving when we met her, but who has not been pleased to see her in these notes selecting, recombining, and inventing? For Patty, language spoken, read, and written will be interwoven in some not-yet-designed manner. She had no trouble with the words in the photo book. She will bring to her new learning a richness already in her mind, once she feels the need.

She will, that is, if school does not dampen her own fire by superimposing some standard, precooked, tasteless method upon her. She has a quiet determination, an inventive and selective mind, and a delight in the world's phenomena which will be protective.

And the ascendent *Greg*. He is now heady with the sense of everything opening up, and he gathers grist for his mill from unlikely fields. (Six blue eggs!) Suddenly he is using the spoken word with meaning and joy. It is my guess that he hears more than his early use of words indicated. His new zest for exploring is affecting his awareness and thus his listening. Some emotional restriction was, I believe, connected with his inability to listen and absorb. Only the months ahead will indicate the extent and the fiber of the coupling.

Greg has so well exemplified how attention is a function of a totality. When well-meaning teachers of "disadvantaged" children speak of training the attention I become irrational. If they were to watch how children bestow their attention when school is relevant and exciting, each child in his own good time and way, they would be as horrified as I to speak of "training" this singularly illusive attribute of living beings. Attention is a close cousin of love, and one does not speak of training someone to love but rather of providing the right setting.

How Greg will fit the written word more significantly into his emerging pattern I cannot say. But with communication opening, as it is, he will seek and find paths if given the chance. I would like to be there as he does. We have seen him travel so far in such a brief time.

What of *Janie* who is already one of the favored of this world? To watch her through these notes—to be with her—is to feel warmth in the joy and goodness which one small human being radiates. Such a child needs less from us professionally than most. She is indeed on her way, and will take the best from any reasonable regime. But knowing this, having verified it often in the past, there still remains a great challenge with these lucky few.

Ad nauseam do our schools point with pride of themselves to children like Janie. It is almost impossible to fail with these children, though mediocre schools do little to stimulate them. Any real teacher measures his worth, any good school measures it, by the width of that margin between what a child brings to school and what he takes from it. Though identification of these margins is not easy, how else can we honestly evaluate our effectiveness? I believe it is mandatory to measure thus if our schools are to become rich places for learning.

It is very difficult to weigh what school has added to Janie's world. She certainly has added to the worlds of other people.

Now we must ask—concerned as we are with schools—how many teachers of our youngest children have the time, the professional encouragement, and small enough classes to release, study, and understand their children's patterns in the early months? Very few, I fear, since so many teachers come to me with pleas for help just here. Yet it is in these first contacts with formal learning that children *not* already on their way must put down roots—deep ones. Too much early "training" is now equated with a "head start." Thus shallow roots are started which depend on mumbo-jumbo memorization of words, narrow patterns of behavior, and that "training" of the attention. Deep roots, of course, may grow coincidentally—signifying that school is sometimes irrelevant. The Janies survive such nonsensical early training *because their deep roots for a more formal learning exist already,* the added shallow roots being accessory only and *not* important.

These six have given us a spring to remember—may it be so for them too.

Those last days! . . . Children early formed the habit of gaining all their images at second hand, by looking at a screen; they grew up believing that anything perceived directly was vaguely fraudulent . . . I think the decline in the importance of direct images dated from the year television managed to catch an eclipse of the moon. After that, nobody ever looked at the sky, and it was as though the moon had joined the shabby company of buskers. There was never really a moment when a child, or even a man, felt free to look away from the television screen—for fear he might miss the one clue that would explain everything.

—E. B. White
The Second Tree from the Corner

Epilogue

□■□■□■□■□■□■□■□■□■□■□■□■□■□■□■□■□■

A brief demonstration proves nothing. It may, however, remind one that there is much that we already know: surely enough to put aside shaking and pummeling, or little rewards suitably administered. Above all, it may suggest that there *is* no single clue, but rather a rich multiplicity and variety to be grasped, to be understood, and to be ordered by priority.

A demonstration may show the meaning of a particular way of ordering, and in this I hope we—six of us very young and very handicapped—have succeeded.

. . . and a picnic with balloons to end our story.

Appendix 1

□■□■□■□■□■□■□■□■□■□■□■□■□■□■□■□■□■□■□■

I shall always be grateful to Dr. Richard Krug for introducing me to these children and for the autonomy he gave me in working with them. With his kind permission the summary of his project is quoted below.

Demonstration Classroom—Language Instruction for the Deaf

The basic purpose of the project is to see if language skills can be developed or improved by concentrating some attention upon the syntactical meaning of words. Special attention upon the syntactical meaning of words might afford a possibility of accelerating the development of language skills of young deaf children. The specific objectives of the demonstration are 1) to teach the syntactical meaning of words at a simple level, 2) to teach the young child of preschool age to write, 3) to allow the child to express himself to some degree, at least, without writing, without speech, finger spelling, or signing. The approach of the demonstration was to program information and the development of ideas in an effort to have the children come to understand the function of a word within a specific sentence structure. The original intent was to utilize a color code in an attempt to identify classes of words but such color coding was found to be unnecessary. Observation of the preschool group revealed that with appropriate programming of ideas three- and four-year-old deaf children can come to understand the syntactical meaning of words as demonstrated by their ability to construct, read, and react appropriately to the vocabulary presented to them and used within specific sentence structures. The approach, technique, and materials developed during the first year of the project will be utilized in five different schools for the deaf in the United States during the coming school year. The original demonstration group will then be used to develop the techniques and approaches for the second year of language development.

Appendix 2

□■□■□■□■□■□■□■□■□■□■□■□■□■□■□■□■□■□■□■

Equipment

This list is a cumulative summary, with comments and additional photographs, of the equipment listed in each chapter. A few items were removed along the way, such as Hamster. It was hard to transport him on cold days, and the children's interest in him diminished as time went on and their interest in manipulative things grew.

The minimal kinds of provisioning we had, especially weak on the biological side, must be thought of in terms of the particular circumstances. We had to trim our sails to the kind of sea and wind we encountered.

In assessing the list, it should also be remembered that the classroom itself provided the blocks, dolls, etc., which the children used, I assume, on other days.

Two important addresses for ordering equipment: Elementary Science Study, Education Development Center, 55 Chapel St., Newton, Mass. 02158; Edmund Scientific Co., 100 Edscorp Bldg., Barrington, N.J. 08007—catalogue on request with magnets, prisms, hand lenses, flashlight-magnifiers, gels, etc.

Hamster: in small cage, with sunflower seeds, celery, lettuce, etc, for him to eat. See *Gerbils,* a small suggestive booklet published by the Elementary Science Study. Watch for *Don't Have Animals in the Classroom—Unless,* available soon from Mountain View Center, 1511 University Ave., Campus, University of Colorado, Boulder, Colo. 80302.

Bubble Equipment: straws, small cans, Ivory Snow, glycerine. Proportions of soap and water vary with the hardness of local water. We used 2–4 teaspoons of glycerine per quart of soap solution. It makes longer lasting bubbles. The skin of threes and fours is sensitive enough to suggest soap rather than detergent, though the latter, suitably diluted, is acceptable for older children. With older children there is much investigation to be done on the properties of bubble mixes (e.g., size and durability of bubbles), as these vary with proportions in the mix and with the kinds of soap or detergent used.

Tire Tubes and Pump: with the valve stem covers which are slotted on the ends to make a little wrench for removing or replacing the valve. We find that both bicycle and automobile tubes are valuable. A bicycle tube develops an enlarged "balloon" easily, which is comical and instructive. A good supply of the elusive valve stem caps is necessary since they are so small. One needs them to let the air out quickly. The pump is a standard automobile tire pump and can be obtained from automobile supply shops.

Large Transparent Plastic Syringes: These can be bought from hospital supply companies in various sizes. We used 50 cc.

Transparent Rigid Plastic Tubes: are available in plastics stores in a variety of diameters and weights, and may be cut to desired lengths by the supplier or with a hacksaw. The ends can be sandpapered to remove cutting burrs and to round edges. A good supply of corks, in assorted sizes, was provided.

Attribute Blocks: These are a set of 75 colored 1-inch cubes, and a set of 32 pieces of four shapes, four colors, and two sizes, with colored nylon loops. They can be obtained from Elementary Science Study. See picture on page 140.

Flashlight-Magnifier: This was a small, expensive one with a rechargeable battery. There are larger and less expensive ones on the market which use standard flashlight cells. The fixed focus plus light make these useful for small children, but they do not replace hand lenses or thread counters (linen-tester lenses), which can be obtained from Edmund Scientific Co.

Flashlights: See Visit 4 for discussion of the need for batteries, bulbs, wires, and sockets. (A *daily* check and discarding of any dead batteries is necessary.)

Food Colors: For a whole school these can be bought dry from grocery or bakery supply houses and dissolved as needed. In this form they are very cheap per unit of solution. Large bottles of food color are on the shelves of most markets which, for young children, can be diluted about 10 to 1. The color is less intense when spilled, yet deep enough to make vivid clouds in water.

Holding Place for Water: These are Pueblo Indian words; we have nothing so appropriate. Any large tub or plastic wading pool will do. For small children there is some advantage to having it low. Expensive water tables are available. See picture on page 138.

Gels: Books with 44 different shadings and colors can now be bought from Edmund Scientific Co. They call these *Color Filter Books.* Each filter page in the size we find most convenient is 5 x 8 inches. Cut each filter to make four gels 2 x 5 inches—big enough to see through—no waste. Taped edges and rounded corners protect children's eyes and the gels themselves. These are best described by the pictures on page 79. The name of the color was printed on the tape and in a "table of contents" on a large sturdy envelope fixed with a yarn shoulder strap:

LISA'S 6 GELS

1 BLUE GEL

1 RED GEL

(etc.)

Dilution Trays: These molded trays (used by pharmacists and other diluters) have 8 x 12 or so small depressions (marble size) and come from a plastics store among other places. By some mail shopping we found it possible to get free "seconds." We have now found trays with larger holes (36), which I recommend. They are called "dental" trays. The cost is small, and plastics outlets sell them. See picture on page 140.

Eyedroppers (Bulb Pipettes): One can find these made of plastic at drugstores, but the milkiness of the plastic prevents a clear view of the color drawn into the pipette. In general, I do not recommend using glass equipment with young children, but with the small size and careful use here, I have found glass to be satisfactory. Clear plastic droppers would be better but I have found none. Transparency invites observation of the effect of a squeeze or release and this is important for exploring the feedback of delicate control. Stick to plastic—if you can.

Thin Aluminum Containers: These were large, old fashioned salt shakers. We filled them with a variety of materials: pebbles, beans, peas, rice, sunflower seeds, lead shot, sand. When shaken, the sounds are subtly characteristic of the material inside. Yet even without sound there are clues from heft and vibration. See picture on page 140.

Clear Plastic Containers With Caps: Ours were large discarded pill bottles, cylinders about 2 x 5 inches and filled with the same materials as above. Pictures and text show the ways in which the children used them. I have since used these and the aluminum containers and contents with kindergarteners. They are stimulating in a variety of ways: for guessing, for reading, for feeling. See picture on page 140.

Things to Take Apart and Put Together: A good junkyard is well worth spending time in to search for such materials. We found large nuts and bolts, old box cameras, an old alarm clock (with alarm still working), and much more. The cost was minimal.

Paper Towels: For painting on and dropping color on. It is a decent material to take the place—for the youngest—of filter paper or chromatography paper.

Playdough: The usual mixture, about 2 parts of flour to 1 of salt, with color and water enough to make it look and feel right. This is too expensive and not as versatile as good clay, but it is useful in emergencies or as a special kind of modeling material—with older children, for example, for making relief maps.

Periscope Prism: Army surplus shops still have these, cheap enough and well encased in metal so that breakage is difficult. These should not, of course, replace ordinary prisms.

Balances: The kind I use here is best described in the picture of Phillip, page 100. The sturdy base sat on the floor. There was a finishing nail in the upright for a fulcrum, put in at a slight angle to prevent the crossarm from constantly slipping off. Many holes were drilled in the crossarm yardstick so that cups could be suspended in different places and the stick itself balanced or unbalanced. I chose the yardstick not because of its numbers but because it was easy to scale and drill. Paper cups were hung on at random by means of pipe cleaners. In the small box which went with each balance was a collection of lightweight junk, of different sizes, shapes, and densities: paper clips of different sizes, golf tees of different colors, styrofoam balls, marbles, metal chain, etc.

In my own classroom for the young I try to have a wide variety of balances, from the kind described here to a simple board, 1 x 6 inches x 3 feet, on a rounded fulcrum, seesaw variety. Some have used a large walk-on and sit-on variety with a low fulcrum. This requires more teacher-involvement than I wanted here. I tried it one day for a few minutes, but removed it to save fingers and toes and ankles from being squeezed. See *The Balance Book,* Elementary Science Study. Think through the scaling of weights according to sensitivity and size of balance.

Colored Chalk and Wet Construction Paper: See Visit 11 and picture, page 141.

Pegboard, Rods, and Bolts: See description and pictures in Visit 12.

Plastic Water Jugs: Two-gallon size, with two capped holes at top. See picture below. Clear plastic whisky jugs now available in multi-gallon size.

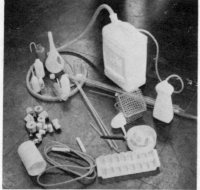

Colored gels:
to hold
to look at
to see through

. . . after seeing through!

Clear Flexible Plastic Tubing: Comes in many diameters and has many uses, from siphons to talking-tubes. Sold by the foot at plastics stores. (One can use plastic tubes from cheap jump ropes.)

Pulleys: I have yet to find a child who does not take to the pulley as something he has "always wanted to use." Our children here were no exception. The wheel, of course, is not always necessary. A five-year-old found this out recently when the pulley wheel we were using came out of the ceiling. By the time we got the ladder to replace it he had looped the rope, with a stuffed ball on one end, over a curtain rod: "Look, I made a pulley myself!"

Plastic Containers: of all sizes, with tops. One relies on one's friends to save them, in many useful shapes and sizes—clear if possible.

Et Cetera: We brought a good supply of rags, extra containers, colored paper, colored chalk, soap, funnels, and other odds and ends as accessories to the equipment listed above.

Water: From week to week minor changes were made in equipment for the water play. The pictures give a sample selection of the "junk" for water: detergent squeeze bottles, old plastic medicine jars, berry baskets, funnels, the plastic water carrier, plastic tubes, etc. What to remove or to add, of course, was often suggested by the children's inventive use of what was provided. Janie found blowing-at-long-distance irresistible one morning, so we opened the camera while closing our eyes to the hygienic implications, and next time brought an extra supply of soap.

When Patty (see pages 71–72) took a dry pea and later a sunflower seed from the shaker stuff and dropped them into her water-filled tube, we were reminded that marbles for children to use in the tubes might add a new dimension.

Diameters came center stage as the joy and concentration of the children in fitting corks to tube ends became evident. We added a wider variety of diameters, so that the children could further enjoy matching and gauging.

Shakers: These are the aluminum and plastic shakers. The peas, beans, rice, rocks, etc. have their own contrasting attributes. What is rather startling is that many of these can be discerned, by sound or feel, through the thin walls of the aluminum shakers. For older children the sieves with graduated mesh offer possibilities for sorting and discovering other characteristics of these materials.

Screwdrivers

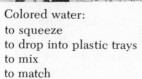

Attribute Blocks:
to sort by color, size, or shape
to count—to build or play guessing games wi
(Further description on p. 134.)

Colored water:
to squeeze
to drop into plastic trays
to mix
to match

Chalk and Blackboard: The top picture was taken on the first day
of picture taking (and about the last in which a child would take
time out for watching the process—as Greg and Janie do here.)
After a morning of blowing bubbles and watching them rise in the
sealed tubes, chalk and blackboard easily communicated these
new words and their recently meaningful adjectives. The "little

Mouths   Gels

Pumps

Watered paper—
Colored chalk

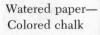

bubble" being drawn in the picture amused Patty, Brooke, and Lisa enough that they subsequently took chalk and made many tiny "bubbles" on the board for each other's enjoyment.

Pegs
and
Holes

Bolts and
nuts
Hands
Fingers
Sticks

and Time
and Thought

Partial Bibliography

□■□■□■□■□■□■□■□■□■□■□■□■□■□■□■□■□■□■

Allen, Frederick H. *Positive Aspects of Child Psychiatry.* New York: W. W. Norton & Co., 1963.

Allen, Frederick H. *Psychotherapy with Children.* New York: W. W. Norton & Co., 1942.

Boys, C. V. *Soap Bubbles: Their Colors and Forces Which Mold Them.* New York: Dover Publications, 1959.

Escalona, Sibylle K. *The Roots of Individuality: Normal Patterns of Development in Infancy.* Chicago: Aldine Publishing Co., 1968.

Gorky, Maxim. *My Childhood.* London: Oxford University Press, 1961.

Helfer, Ray E., M.D., and Kempe, C. Henry, M.D. *The Battered Child.* Chicago: University of Chicago Press, 1968.

Helfer, Ray E., M.D., and Kempe, C. Henry, M.D. *Helping the Battered Child and His Family.* Philadelphia: J. B. Lippincott Co., 1972.

Hilgard, Ernest R., *Theories of Learning.* New York: Appleton-Century-Crofts, Inc., 1956.

James, Henry. *What Maisie Knew.* New York: Doubleday & Co., Anchor Books, 1954.

Lenneberg, Eric H. *Biological Foundations of Language.* New York: John Wiley and Sons, 1967.

Piaget, Jean. *Studies in Education: First Years in School.* London: Evans Bros., published for the Institute of Education, University of London, 1963.

Psychoanalytic Study of the Child. New York: International Universities Press, 1945–1969: Freud, Anna. "Child Observation and Prediction of Development," Discussion by R. A. Spitz, H. Hartmann, R. Waelder. Vol. 13 (1958a), p. 92124; Freud, Anna. "Discussion of Dr.

John Bowlby's Paper." Vol. 15 (1960), pp. 53–62; Freud, Anna, and Dann, S. "An Experiment in Group Upbringing." Vol. 6 (1951), pp. 127–69; Spitz, R. A., and Wolf, Katherine. "Autoerotism: Some Empirical Findings and Hypotheses on Three of its First Manifestations in Life." Vols. 3–4 (1949), pp. 85–120.

Richardson, Elwyn S. *In the Early World*. New York: Pantheon Books, 1964.

Tolstoy, Leo. "On Methods of Teaching the Rudiments." In *On Education*. Chicago: University of Chicago Press, 1967.

ABOUT THE AUTHOR

Frances Pockman Hawkins is codirector (with her husband) of the Mountain View Center for Environmental Education at the University of Colorado in Boulder. For many years, she has been a teacher of young children and a trainer of teachers, in Nigeria, Kenya, and Uganda as well as in the United States.